Mom
'06

Get a
Bigger Wagon

written by
Maureen Haddock

paintings by
Denyse Klette

Published in Canada in 2005
Trek 2000 Corporation
65 Cathedral Bluffs Road
Saskatoon, SK S7P 1A3

Library and Archives Canada Cataloguing in Publication

Haddock, Maureen, 1949-
    Get a bigger wagon / Maureen Haddock ; Denyse Klette, illustrator.

ISBN 0-9732032-1-8

    1. Haddock, Gord, 1949- -Childhood and youth-Anecdotes.
2. Saskatchewan-Social life and customs-20th century-Anecdotes.
I. Klette, Denyse, 1963- II. Title.

FC3525.1.H34H33 2005   C818'.602   C2005-905315-1

This book is a celebration of the entrepreneurial spirit,
and of the province of Saskatchewan
where diverse experiences are available
for those born with such spirit.

I salute the parents and the grandparents who
strive to find the right compromise in raising
fiercely independent children.

Jarrett, this one's for you!

Preface

The stories in this book are meant to be read randomly. They are a collection, placed in no particular order. Enjoy them, like a conversation around the kitchen table, with one story triggering another. Read them out loud to your grandchildren and your siblings. Hopefully, your listeners will interrupt you with stories of their own.

These stories are inspired by my husband's detailed memories about growing up in small town Saskatchewan during the nineteen fifties. At the end of each story, I include what I think he learned from the experience. Then, I share what he thinks he learned. Since he is an entrepreneur, it is what he thinks he learned that really matters.

The introductory story "Beyond the Line" was inspired by conversations I have had with my mother-in-law. The boy has no memory of the incidents in this introductory story but his free spirit was apparent even at this early age. It is possible that she was the ideal mother for the fiercely independent boy. In this story, she learns that there is a fine line between squelching a child's independent nature and letting him run wild. I think she did a great job of the compromise.

Beyond the Line

The boy had celebrated his second birthday that summer. He was a busy curious child who could play for long periods by himself. His mother knew his independent nature required a watchful eye. On a sunny fall morning in the early fifties, the boy's mother was feeling weary. Wrapping her cardigan tightly around her body, she sat on the cold and crumbling front step. The sun bounced off the colorful leaves right into her eyes and she put up her hand to create shade. She felt the slightest warmth from the sun's rays, but it was no match for the penetrating cold of the late fall.

Her older son had left for school and the breakfast dishes were washed but there was a stew to prepare for the pot, clothes to scrub by hand, fallen leaves to rake and shirts to iron. She had to do everything without losing sight of her toddler and that meant the tasks took longer.

She smiled weakly as she remembered the promise she had made to her husband some months ago. She agreed to move with him from the city in the East where roads were paved, water ran from taps and neighbor women shared the sometimes lonely task of childrearing. Here in the small prairie town, she knew her husband had a chance to fulfill his entrepreneurial dreams. She believed the small town would provide a wonderful place to raise her sons. Having made the decision to move, she hadn't looked back.

Today she watched her son digging happily in the dirt, moving trucks and animals in a labyrinth of his own creation. She admired his concentration and contentment. He had a beautiful spirit and she wanted him to grow to his full potential.

Just as she began to relax for the first time in days, the coal truck pulled up and impatiently beeped its horn. She hated the black film that coated everything after the coal was dumped into her house. The arrival of the season's first order of coal marked the beginning of winter. She knew she had to run inside to make sure the doors to the coal bin and basement were closed tight. Keeping the black dust confined was impossible but she had to try. In the East, their little flat had been heated with oil.

The little boy ran toward the big truck greeting the driver with a friendly wave. As the driver leapt from his vehicle and headed to the house to undo the flap on the coal chute, he stopped for a moment to tousle the boy's matted hair and ask about his day. The boy smiled up at the delivery man.

The mother knew she had to hurry in to tend to the doors. Had the boy been in his harness she would have been able to tether him to the clothesline as she sometimes did. The long leash allowed him to have the run of the yard without being in danger while she worked. She had developed this idea when they moved into the little rented house, which stood without fences, on a corner bordered by two busy roads. One of the roads was edged by a very deep ditch which in spring, often filled with water. She had to protect the boy from his own curiosity.

She knew she had only a minute before the coal dust would fill her house. With the harness not in sight, she decided to tie one end of a rope to the cross formed by the overall straps on the boy's back. The other end she would tie to the clothesline. That done, she ran inside to close the doors. She'd only be gone for a moment.

As she walked through the basement she took in the sight of it all. The hopper to the furnace held three or four pails of coal, and because of its size, only needed to be filled a couple of times a day. She had never imagined that coal shoveling would take a prominent place among the many tasks that consumed her time. Her husband worked long hours to nurture their new business and many tasks fell to her. Slowly a smile brightened her tired face and she felt a tiny spark of pride for handling it all.

Outside again, she spoke with the coal man regarding the billing for this delivery. The coal was dumped into her house. There was small talk about the beautiful fall leaves and the sun-filled day and then he hopped into the truck and backed into the street. As he did this, she instinctively glanced to the yard to be sure the boy was far away from the truck's wheels.

As her eyes casually surveyed the yard, her chest tightened and she was unable to breathe. Slowly her legs moved toward the clothesline. There, hanging as if freshly washed, was an empty pair of overalls. The boy, determined to explore beyond his boundaries, had simply slid out of his pants.

Get a Bigger Wagon

She left the yard and looked up both streets knowing he couldn't have gone far. It had only been a minute, yet there was no sign of him. As she walked, she told her story to every townsperson she met. Finally, she went to the store to tell her husband that their son was momentarily missing. Customers overheard her words and one man made a phone call. In a matter of minutes, someone in the town office clamped the loudspeaker onto the top of a car and began driving up and down Main Street announcing that a boy was missing. The description, although accurate, was unnecessary. Most of the citizens knew the boy.

Reports of sightings of the boy began to come in immediately. Minutes later, the manager of the hardware store crossed the street to invite the mother to see firsthand, where her son was playing. Gingerly, she entered the store. The manager directed her to the back, where there were several tricycles of all sizes on display. The boy sat happily in his underpants, on the smallest one, unaware of the concern and anguish he had caused his mother. He chatted happily to shoppers, repeating words like: wheels, pedals, and mine.

As she walked toward her son, relief swept over her. The boy, unaware of her presence, spun around smiling cheerfully, when she hugged him from behind. The boy's mother whispered something in his ear about getting off the tricycle and heading for home because his big brother would be expecting lunch.

As they walked to the door of the store, she realized she was energized by the love she had felt from the citizens of the little town. Everyone had been caring and helpful. She thought she could hear dramatic music. The rich notes swept her away. She allowed herself to imagine being greeted by a crowd of well-wishers. She would leave the store, triumphant, her small son in her arms. There would be a band playing and certainly there would be streamers and cheering onlookers! Everyone would be happy for her. She had often, since the move, felt like she was in a movie.

Back in the real world, she left the store to begin her walk home. She admitted to herself that the boy was always going to follow his heart. Her job would simply be, to help him grow wise enough to do it safely. She came to another realization that day as well. This really was the best place she could think of to raise this boy.

Contents

Moving a Mountain

It was spring in a small Saskatchewan town and the boy and his friend had spent a delightful morning looking for tadpoles or any sign of early slough life. Although they followed the highway east of town, they actually spent most of their time in the water-filled ditches. In the morning, the water was still solid around the edges and the boys enjoyed the sharp cracking sound as their boots broke through the ice and the slow swoosh as their feet were sucked into the frigid water below. The smell of the thawing dead grasses was so strong it left a bitter taste on their tongues.

Their plan was to find some old boards and build a raft to float on the slough. They were in no hurry. As they neared the swamp their eyes skillfully scanned the area for materials that would be of use in this project. Then the day took a more urgent turn. There, just ahead, emanating from the base of a telephone pole was a beam of light that seemed to pulse and move as though inviting the boys to investigate. This, was something important!

Peeking from beneath the wet grasses was a rock, glinting with gold. To reach the treasure, the boys walked through water, deep enough to seep over their boot tops. They began to dig with sticks around the exposed rock. As they scraped away the thawing mud and wet grass they reached frozen ground and still there was more of the gold laced rock to unearth. Furiously, they scraped and pried at the rock, their hearts beating rapidly from excitement and exertion. The rock was as big as a basketball! Their eyes were large with the understanding that they had found gold! The only place to get a fair appraisal of such a find would be at the local jewelry store.

Each boy bent to lift one side of the rock and together they successfully held the precious prize between them. Within seconds, they realized that they would never be able to get it to town this way. They would need to get the wagon. They put the rock back in place and covered it with mud and grass before setting off for town to retrieve the friend's wagon.

The walk to town and back was made short with their dreaming and planning. They retraced their steps and quickly found the rock beneath the planted debris. Once again, they lifted the treasure together and this time placed it carefully into the clear water beyond the telephone pole, to rinse it off. As they lifted the glistening wet rock from the water to place it in the wagon, their excitement was renewed. The boy removed his jacket and placed it reverently over the rock so as to conceal it from other's curiosity and they began the journey back to town. They were sure the jeweler would be very impressed and want to buy their rock!

They pulled the wagon into the south end of town, past the elevators and on to Main Street, where the friend stood guard beside the rock while the boy went into the store to talk to the jeweler. Inside, there was much gesturing and head bobbing before the boy and the jeweler came out to view the prize.

The discussion was something about the size of the rock and the fact that the gold was in the form of tiny flakes. There was an explanation about how very many such rocks it would take to produce enough gold to create jewelry. There was no mention of the term "fool's gold." The jeweler did acknowledge that it was a mighty fine rock and had been a lot of work to retrieve. The jeweler thought a while, scratched his head a bit, stroked his chin and then he told the boys that he'd be willing to give them a whole dollar for the rock. The boys were expecting that such a rock would fetch a greater price, but still, a dollar was a lot of money.

And so, exhausted from a day of walking, hauling, dreaming and negotiating they set off for the comfort of their respective homes to eat and rest and think about the day's adventure and what each would do with his fifty cents.

I have watched my husband expend more energy on projects than warranted. The look of hope and excitement on his face during the work has always been reward enough for me. When I asked him what he learned from the adventure with the rock, he laughed and said, "I learned that you should do the research before you do the grunt work." Then he added, "I learned from the jeweler that life's real gold often comes in the form of kindness and generosity from others."

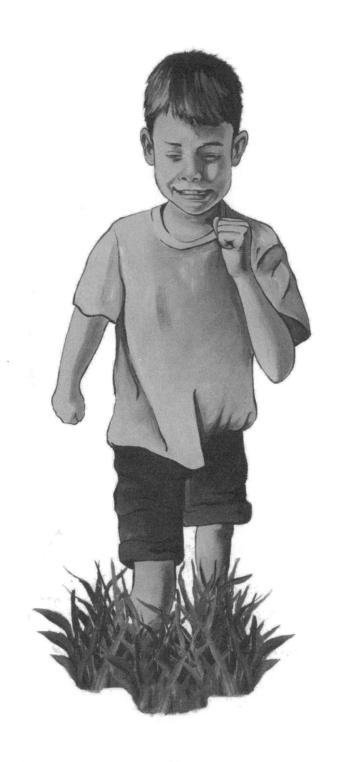

The Drayman

It was one of those mornings in the fifties, in small town Saskatchewan, when the snow was almost gone and the gumbo clay roads smelled of dampness. The air was crisp and cool yet the early morning sun felt warm on the cheeks. The little boy left his house with a full stomach of cereal and orange juice and began the walk to his friend's home. The sun occasionally bounced off a puddle of water right into the little boy's eyes, making him squint and contort his smooth little face until he resembled the adventurer he perceived himself to be.

His friend was ready when he knocked on the door. Both boys were wearing flannel shirts that offered cozy protection from the spring winds. Their blue jeans were tucked into rubber boots that rose right to the creases in the backs of their knees. As always, the friend's red wagon was in tow, just in case they came upon a valuable rock or an animal in need of help.

The two set out enthusiastically, chatting constantly as they headed toward the north end of town. They traveled through back alleys, backyards and water-filled ditches, always looking for something to investigate. It was fun for them to let the gumbo collect in large blocks on the bottom of their boots and then wade gingerly into frigid water-filled ditches to dissolve the clay. Their feet could scarcely tell the feeling of cold from wet.

Get a Bigger Wagon

Suddenly, their adventure began. Just off the alley, right in front of them, was a huge garage with its doors open wide. This garage was filled to bursting with bottles! The boys looked at each other and without speaking gathered up at least four cases that seemed to be slightly outside the garage, tucked them into the red wagon and hastily began their retreat. Just as they turned to leave, a deep voice shouted, "Hey, what are you boys doing?"

The man gave chase and the two boys headed out as fast as their rubber boots would allow. They ran down the alley stumbling forward in their haste with one boy pulling the wagon and the other steadying the bottles. In spite of the substantial size of this man, he seemed to be gaining on them. The boys knew they would have to leave the wagon. They hoped he would stop to retrieve his bottles giving them time to get away.

Free of the wagon, but filled with adrenalin from the fear of being caught, they continued to run through the north end of town past the park and on to the downtown area. They didn't stop there! They ran several blocks to the Esso Gas Station on the highway and on into the field where they approached a dugout. They slid to the inside edge of the dugout, pressing their tummies onto the damp ledge, leaving only the tops of their heads and their eyes peeking over to keep watch.

At first they lay very still, perhaps hoping to become part of the bank. Their flannel shirts were wet from the sweat of terror, excitement and the relief of having escaped capture. It was a long time before they ventured out of their hiding place. The sun was high and hot and their stomachs were empty. The two decided to go home to the friend's house for lunch.

The walk was long but enjoyable. They felt safe and secure that their identities were unknown. For a while they even allowed themselves to be a bit giddy about the whole incident.

As they rounded the corner to the friend's house, they realized the adventure wasn't over just yet. There, on the step to the house, sat the drayman. He, of course, owned the bottles they had collected from near his garage. He, of course, paid people to give them to him for resale. He motioned for the boys to sit down on the step beside him.

The drayman's talk was something about stealing and where that can lead a boy and something about keeping this between them, as men. The part that stuck with the boys the most, was that if they were really in need, they should just ask for help but never should they steal.

The lesson was sinking in. Still, the boys were confused as to how the man had discovered who they were and even where one of them lived. They had to ask. The drayman rose and gave a stern look at each of them. It was clear that this had been a very serious morning. Then he slowly raised his hand and pointed one gnarly finger towards the name and address written inside the wagon.

Get a Bigger Wagon

During our years in business, my husband often gave some-one a second chance by keeping a shoplifting incident between those involved. He often made it clear to them that if they were in need, they should ask, but never take. When I asked him what else he might have learned from this incident, he smiled and said, "Well, if you are going to do something silly, at least don't leave your calling card."

Too Many Rules

It was a sunny fall morning, in the small Saskatchewan town and the street where the boy lived was hemmed on each side by a perfectly even mound of fallen leaves. He ran through them making swishing crunching sounds. He pulled his toque down over his ears. His mother had been right; it was quite chilly. He spent a moment trying to make patterns with the steam emerging from his mouth.

It had been lonely on the street since the children in the neighborhood went back to school. He was the only pre-school child on the block. Today he planned to go to school with the others. The children in his neighborhood were heading toward the old brick building. He caught up to them as they crossed the last street into the schoolyard.

He watched with interest as the boys pulled small bags of shiny marbles from their pockets. One boy drew a large circle in the powdery dirt with his heal. Two girls twirled a rope while others skipped. Some children played ball while others climbed up the poles that supported the swings. When the school bell impatiently jangled, the games stopped abruptly, and the boy was moved along with the other children in a sea of motion.

Inside the school, he took off his coat and hung it on a hook, as the other boys did. He watched as the children slid into desks and then he sat down in one that contained no books. The teacher called out each child's name and made a mark in a long thin yellow book. He sat quietly as she ceremoniously pressed the blotter onto the page to dry the ink. When she looked up, he wondered if she noticed him. She began her lesson.

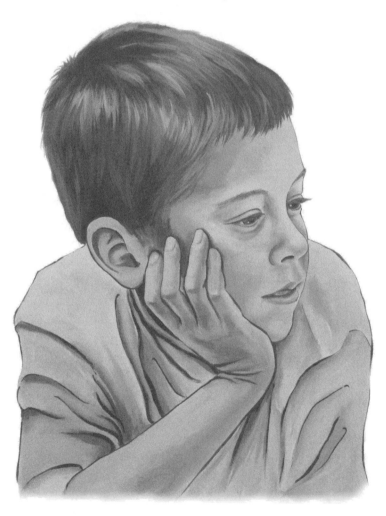

The morning had been interesting enough. They watched a film strip and searched for cities on the big pull-down map. Recess was hardly long enough to set up a game much less play one. The jangling bell interrupted everything. He noticed that the children responded to the bell immediately whenever they heard it. They didn't seem to mind the sound. After lunch, he chose to play by himself, on the big empty street where he lived.

The boy continued to attend school whenever he felt lonely. Each time he went missing from the street, his mother would arrive at the school to collect him. She would exchange knowing glances with the teacher, usher the boy out the door, and smile patiently. The women had talked about the boy and decided he was going through a phase that would surely pass, if little was made of it.

One morning while the boy was at school, the super-intendent came for a visit. It was that day, before lunch, that the teacher had a chat with the boy. Apparently, there were rules about who could go to school and who couldn't. He would need to wait another year for the privilege. When the teacher gently added that she had enjoyed his visits, he looked down, shrugged his small shoulders and walked slowly home.

Months passed and summer came and the street was once again busy with children. The small boy enjoyed each day, forgetting about school and superintendents. The street was bright and noisy with children. Parents stopped to talk to each other as they worked in the yards. The delicious smell of barbequed food frequently filled the street. Then, one day, the boy noticed there were leaves on the driveway.

Fall had arrived and he was officially old enough to join everyone at school. The playground looked the same, the bell jangled in the same urgent manner and the children responded in one giant mass. Inside the school, jackets were hung on the same hooks. There was a new teacher. She seemed nice. This time his name was called and a mark was made just for him, in the big yellow book.

The morning went well but the recess was as short as he remembered. There was no time for a proper game. When the awful bell rang to call them back to class, he decided to walk home. He played in the yard near his house, enjoying the quiet and the cool air. His mother walked from the house and kneeled to speak with him. The school had phoned and she was to take him back. There were rules about attending. It occurred to the boy, as they walked toward the school, that the same superintendent that told him he couldn't attend last year, was responsible for making him go this year.

He didn't mind school; he even liked his teacher. He just felt it was wrong to make someone stay somewhere, when they wanted to be somewhere else. He felt that superintendents, whoever they were, made too much fuss about everything.

That fall, he left school many times. He walked in the fields and hid in the culverts, where there were no bells. Sometimes, he played in the bushes on the outskirts of town, for long uninterrupted afternoons. His attendance record on that first report card was very poor. His mother was sure this stage would pass. Deep inside, she actually knew how he felt. The teacher welcomed him warmly on days when he attended. She too, seemed to understand. He was the topic of discussion among teachers and relatives. What should they do about the boy?

As fall turned into winter and the days grew cold and dark, he chose to stay at school more often. He had projects to finish and friends to visit. He developed the skill of having adventures inside his mind. He could plan quietly for the weekend or for after school. He could see himself winning at marbles or finding treasures. His next report card praised his notably improved attendance record, but mentioned a definite tendency to daydream.

The boy gradually adapted to school life. Still, getting used to something didn't make it right.

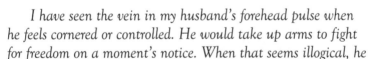

I have seen the vein in my husband's forehead pulse when he feels cornered or controlled. He would take up arms to fight for freedom on a moment's notice. When that seems illogical, he simply withdraws into his mind to freely make a new plan.

When I asked my husband what he learned from his early school experiences, he concluded that he likely hadn't learned too much, because he said, "Admittedly, I'm still that boy."

Abrupt Ending

It was a sunny day in early spring, in the small Saskatchewan town. The boy leaned against the house, enjoying the heat from the siding. He was waiting for one of his friends to pick him up in a new Ford Ranchero. The friend's father, excited about his new vehicle, had offered to drive them out to the creek to go tobogganing. The boys wondered, since it was so warm, if the dad would let them ride in the open back of the sleek vehicle; half car and half truck. After some begging and whining, the boys were allowed to climb into the back, where they learned first hand about how cold the spring air feels as it rushes past you at sixty miles an hour.

The boys often tobogganed down the creek hills but when they arrived at their usual site, they were disappointed to find melted circles everywhere. The best hill faced south and with the increased tobogganing activity of spring, the paths were worn thin. The rocks, now exposed, retained heat from the sun and melted everything around them. The friend's father noticed the boys' disappointed faces and suggested that they try the country roads.

After a few minutes of driving in the country, they came to a stop. Since these roads were rarely traveled, the father allowed himself to develop an idea. He grabbed a long rope from the back of the truck and he tied one end to the toboggan and the other to the trailer hitch. He gestured to the toboggan and told the boys to climb on. The boy sat close behind his bigger friend, wrapping his arms and legs around him. Their enormous eyes revealed their utter astonishment at what was happening.

The father explained that he could see them in the rear view mirror at the side of the truck because the rope was really long. He told them he would drive carefully and they would have a ride to remember. As he put the vehicle in gear, he shouted through the open window, something about being sure to wave if they wanted him to stop. Looking in the mirror, he waved at them and the games began.

For many miles, the boys laughed and encouraged the dad to go faster. When the speed increased, the boys laughed shrilly, like patrons of a mid-way. A tingling sensation buzzed through their limbs whenever they hit a bump or took a curve too fast. The boys were relieved that they could see the father in the side mirror, like he promised. The frigid wind whizzed past their cheeks and their stomachs filled with nervous excitement, but stopping wasn't an option. This chance might never come again.

As the truck hugged the curves of the country roads, the friend clutched the front of the toboggan and the boy clung to the back of his friend. As the Ranchero turned to the right, the toboggan was thrown to the left side of the road. When the truck went left, the boys found themselves on the right. They learned to lean into those turns. It was like playing a really fast game of crack-the-whip.

Abrupt Ending

At the end of one very long wide sweep to the left, the father lost sight of the boys. The boy and his friend had no time to wonder where the truck had gone because the rope had popped off the ball of the trailer hitch, and the toboggan continued with great speed on its trajectory.

The toboggan catapulted off the road, skimmed over the ditch, bounced once and then drilled itself straight into a huge snowbank, at least eight-feet tall. Onlookers, had there been any, would have thought this was a scene from a Road Runner cartoon. Unlike Wile E. Coyote, who would have slammed into a mountain and slid disoriented to its base, the boy's friend was in too far to slide to safety. The boy sat on the back half of the toboggan, which stuck out of the bank like a huge tongue.

For a moment, neither boy moved. They were stunned. All the boy could see of his friend was the back of his body, an inlaid image looking almost painted onto the bank. There was a weak and muffled sound from inside the snow. In response, the boy began to dig his own legs out. He shimmied his way to the back of the toboggan, jumped off, and began to dig around his friend's body.

When the friend's father had lost sight of the toboggan, he had stopped his vehicle but was unable to turn around on the narrow road. Realizing what had happened, he set out on foot to help the boys. Just as the boy had almost freed his friend, the father arrived to lift his son, sputtering and moaning, from the bank. The friend had snow in his eyes, nostrils, and mouth, as well as inside his ears. It was up his sleeves and in the neck of his jacket. As the boy tried to help his friend, he noticed him struggling for breath. The father and the two boys sat still for a time.

After a moment, they began to walk slowly to the truck. The boy was cold and tired but he felt deep sympathy for his friend. He watched as the big boy wiped away frozen tears with his icy sleeve and stomped angrily toward the truck. The father opened the doors and the boys climbed inside. No one asked to ride in the back this time. Still unable to turn the truck around, the father drove forward to the next grid road and on to another, gradually working his way back to town. The boys and the man rode in silence.

The boy was glad to be home for dinner and when his mother asked him about his day, he told her he had gone out to the creek to toboggan. He mentioned that the season was pretty well finished.

The boy and his friend never again tobogganed behind a vehicle. For that matter, the friend's father never again drove, while pulling a toboggan. As was often the case when things went wrong in the small town, no one spoke about the incident.

I was sure that events such as this, taught my husband to weigh the thrill of an experience against the possible outcome. When I asked him what he learned on this day, he said, "Never tie your success to just one thing. Most sudden stops in life aren't made of snow." Then he added, "I also learned that the second best seat can turn out to be the best!"

Keeping
One's Dignity

It was one of those stiflingly hot days in small town
Saskatchewan, when people gathered in lazy clusters
conversing and mopping their necks and brows with
handkerchiefs. Everywhere there was talk of the weather
and how it was the hottest day in ten years and how in
such heat, you really could fry an egg on the sidewalk.

People were lingering inside the post office because
it was cool there. The boy was doing just that when
he saw his friend bound up the steps toward him, his
friend's sister, not far behind. This friend was excited
because his sister had just received her learner's license!
The boy was impressed because it would be years until
he was old enough for this privilege.

As the three walked toward their homes they developed a plan to cool down. They had a hankering for
soft ice-cream. They were sure they could convince the
friend's grandma to accompany his sister while she
practiced her driving skills. They would all go for a ride
to the Dog 'N' Suds, ten blocks from their street. They
could already feel the cold silky ice-cream sliding down
their parched throats.

Keeping One's Dignity

The friend's grandma was a proper British lady with musical training and wonderful manners. She led choirs and played the organ and even had a live-in house-keeper. The boy had often heard her tell her grand-children to go home and dress for dinner. The friend usually looked well enough dressed but he lived within a few doors of his grandma's house so it wasn't too much trouble to do as she wished. Everyone in the family tried to meet the grandma's expectations.

The friend ran up the stairs, his sister sauntering behind, and asked the grandma about going for ice-cream. Unfortunately, the air-conditioner in the car had broken down so they would have to drive with the windows open. Still, the old woman's eyes twinkled at the thought of having ice-cream on this smoldering hot day. So it was that the boy, his friend, his friend's sister and grandma set out on the hottest day in ten years in an un-air-conditioned luxury car to travel the ten blocks to the Dog 'N' Suds to buy soft ice-cream.

The drive went well. The order was placed and filled with no problems. The boy and his friend sat on respec-tive sides of the enormous back seat, each holding their ice-cream cones. The grandma sat in the passenger seat holding her ice-cream cone in one hand and her grand-daughter's in the other. In the time it took to leave the parking lot the ice-cream had begun to melt.

The boy and his friend enthusiastically licked the sides and the tops of their cones and felt the delicious cool travel down their throats and into their stomachs. They smiled in total satisfaction. Soon they found their tongues could hardly keep up with the torrents of melted ice-cream that spilled over the tops of the cones. The boy and his friend strained to see over the seat where the grandma was sitting. They were amused to notice the ice-cream beginning to run down the backs of her hands. Their eyes met in a silent giggle. As they watched they licked.

The grandma sat posture perfect, looking straight ahead, a cone clutched in each hand. With her thumbs to the tops and little fingers wrapped around the bottoms of the cones, she seemed unaware that the ice-cream had begun to form milky drops on the undersides of her little fingers. The drops under each hand grew too large to fight gravity and they plopped down onto each side of her flowing skirt. As this repeated and repeated, the plops on each side of her skirt began to form streams which flowed from each thigh to the center of her lap. Eventually, this hammock of fabric filled and began to overflow, forming a river aimed directly at her perfectly polished pumps.

Having ignored this predicament for so long and hesitating to lick the ice-cream cones because one belonged to her grand-daughter, she now began to laugh. At first it was a titter and then a giggle and finally, losing complete control, she let out a deep and hearty guffaw. That pressure must have forced a gust of compressed air to discharge itself like a trumpet blast from beneath her skirt. Everyone's eyes grew wide and focused straight ahead, as stunned silence filled the car.

In total quiet, they pulled up to the grandma's house and the friend ran around to the passenger's side to help her out of the car. There was little left of the cones.

There was a new understanding of the term "dress for dinner" because surely she would have to do just that. The boy left for home and the friend began to wipe the car seats clean. The sister was a little disappointed that she didn't get her ice-cream but she was completely satisfied with her good driving.

As time went on, the four of them laughed often about the ice-cream incident but the trumpet sound was never mentioned, even between the boys.

I was sure my husband would tell me that this story taught him to understand the keeping of secrets in order to allow someone her dignity. I even wondered if he might tell me that he learned not to take himself too seriously. However, when I asked my husband what he learned from this incident, he said, "Sometimes things are out of your control and you have to laugh, no matter what the consequences."

The Delayed Dream

In the mid-fifties, in a small Saskatchewan town, the owner of the local hardware store brought in the first three-speed bicycle that the children of the town had ever seen.

One little boy pressed close to the shop window and marveled at the shiny innovative machine. In his mind it was already his. He could feel the wind against his skin as he visualized pedaling with ease up the hill on the other side of the creek.

In a matter of days, he had his plan in place. Sundays became bottle collecting marathons. He'd pull his red wagon for miles in one direction then cross the road to scour the other side for more bottles. It had to happen on Sundays because the bottle supply increased after weekend partying.

On hot days he learned to spend a few minutes in the shadow created by the drive-in movie screen. This was the only shade for miles. The enormous cement pylons that held the screen in place retained the cold from the night and he often spread his small hot body against them. Sometimes he thought he could see the imprint of his body burned into the cement.

One by one the bottles filled his wagon. Load by load the money tallied up. Deposit by deposit his anticipation grew. Each day he added the numbers, estimating how many more Sundays there would be until he could buy his bike.

As he neared his goal he ventured farther from town. On one particular Sunday he planned to go all the way to the three mile corner in order to fill his wagon. He was sure that this was the week the coveted three-speed bike would be his. He set out very early with water and food for the trip. All too soon his wagon was full.

As he turned to come home on the other side of the road, bottles began to slide from the mound he had collected. There were still more bottles to pick up but each time he placed one on top of his pile another fell off and he was forced to stop and rearrange them.

He was traveling ever more slowly, bending over so that one hand could steady the load. At this rate it would take him hours to reach his home. He had to think of a better way to get the job done.

The boy knew he had to remove the excess bottles from the wagon. He glanced about in

search of a place to hide his overstock. His eyes fell
upon the graveyard. Surely his bottles would be safe
there. A thick hedge of caraganas surrounded the area.
He decided to hide his precious inventory deep in their
thick branches.

When the task was complete and he was satisfied
that the bottles were hidden from view, he set off for
home. As he walked he daydreamed about withdrawing
the money, paying for the bike and riding the new three-
speed bicycle everywhere. Tomorrow would be the big
day! He quickened his pace.

Home at last, he unloaded his wagon, ran into his
house, rapidly gulped an entire glass of water and then
drank another. He splashed water on his burning face,
washed his dirty sticky hands with soap and gobbled a
couple of cookies as he darted out the door. In minutes
he was back on the road to retrieve his stash of bottles.

Nearing the graveyard he broke into a run, tipping
his wagon as he excitedly made the sharp turn toward
the hedge. Impatiently, he dragged the wagon along on
its side until he neared the bushes. Then he stopped to
park it upright for easy loading. He breathlessly lifted
branches and then more branches but he could not find
the bottles! He grabbed the branches on either side of
him, thinking he must have made a mistake about the
location. He knew they were there somewhere. Back
and forth he ran, looking, lifting, and repeating the
search. No bottles!

Then the spirit crushing, gut punching reality hit
him. Someone must have seen him hide his extra bottles at the graveyard. While he walked home, someone

Get a Bigger Wagon

took them and delayed his dream. Now he would have to spend another Sunday picking bottles. Worse yet, he would have to wait at least another week to buy his bike!

———————————————————

I have seen that little boy's disappointment in my husband's eyes when people have done business with him in a dishonorable way. It doesn't last long though. True entrepreneurs never give up. Their dreams are never stolen, just delayed. I asked my husband what he learned from that experience. His answer was simply, "Get a bigger wagon."

The Best Seat
in the House

It was six-thirty in the evening on a cold winter night in small town Saskatchewan. Most of the shops were dark within, lit only by the street lights. One small shop was still busy. Through the windows one could see the owner ring the last few purchases through the N.C.R. till. His small son swept the floor carefully and then restocked the empty spots on the shelves, dusting as he did so. Occasionally, the boy looked out the window toward the theatre, now lined up with customers excited about the new movie. He glanced at his watch, back at his father, then hastily packaged the garbage and carted it to the back. Finally, he received the nod from his dad. He grabbed his coat and was off to join the line-up at the theatre.

He was chilly and hungry. His friends were already in the theatre. He assessed the length of the line-up and wondered if the theatre would be full before he made it to the ticket booth. He knew the movie would cost a dime and if he bought a drink, there would be no popcorn. He could smell it already. He yearned for the buttery salty crunch in his mouth.

Finally, he reached the booth. There would be one or two seats left, according to the usher. The usher had worked in the theatre for as long as anyone could remember. His hunched posture and the squeaky voice that escaped from his twisted features made him a mysterious and interesting part of going to the movies. He knew the boy and ushered him into the partial row at the back, reserved for staff. This partial row allowed a storage area for the broom and mop but gave the boy a better view than he'd have in the very front row looking straight up at the screen.

It felt great to sit. He pulled off his boots, took off his coat, stuffed his toque and mitts into one sleeve, took a long sip on his pop and stretched his arm out over the back of the next seat. As his eyes became used to the dark he searched pointlessly for his friends. Oh well, they wouldn't have bothered to save him a seat anyway.

He began to relax, letting his arm drape loosely down the back of the seat. He thought he was dreaming when his hand came to rest on what seemed like a mountain of popcorn. Perhaps it was his imagination. He had reluctantly chosen to buy a drink instead of popcorn, to avoid the torturous thirst that develops from popcorn, with no drink. Now, his hand fondled readily available popcorn. He brought one kernel to his mouth to determine the truth. Miracle of miracles, it was popcorn! They stored the extra popcorn in the partial row. The usher would never miss a few kernels. Oh, lucky day! A seat at the movies, a drink and now an unlimited supply of popcorn was his for the duration of the movie. Surely, life got no better than this.

Get a Bigger Wagon

As the credits rolled and people wiped tears away from their eyes and older kids stopped kissing, the lights came up ever so slowly. The hunched usher took on his other role. Now a custodian, he began the job of sweeping up the spilled popcorn, candy wrappers and drink cups. The boy glanced down at the bin of stored popcorn that had given him such pleasure and noticed to his complete disgust that it also held wrappers, dirt, and drink cups. Just then, the usher dumped a dustpan full of debris from the back row, into the bin. The boy didn't have to ask. He knew he had been eating floor sweepings all night.

When I asked my husband what he learned from the popcorn incident all he said was, "If it seems too good to be true, it is!"

No Contract

There were chores that the boy was obliged to do. His parents believed everyone in a family had to make a contribution. Sometimes, the snow-removal chore caused a little friction between the boy and his mother. To keep this friction to a minimum, she would simply inform the boy that the snow had to be removed from the driveway before bedtime. Given that he had the whole day to complete this task, he usually elected to begin about fifteen minutes before his deadline. This meant he was forced to hurriedly shovel heavy snow, in the coldest darkest part of the winter day. Still, there was satisfaction in actually choosing the last available time.

One Saturday in the early spring, the boy awoke to a snowfall so pure and huge that the roof lines of the street appeared sculpted from Styrofoam. The sun was sparkling off the snow and he sat on the hot air vent in his flannel pajamas, smiling at the whimsical view.

The boy jumped when the phone rang. It was one of his friends with a great idea for making some quick cash. The friend suggested that they each get busy and clear their own sidewalks because they would need to shovel themselves out of their doors anyway. Then, they should bring their family shovels and together offer to clear people's sidewalks for money. They agreed that they had to get started before this great opportunity melted.

Get a Bigger Wagon

The boy ate an extra piece of toast and washed it down with orange juice, then dressed himself in all of his winter gear. The thick beige parka went on over his navy waterproof pants which were tucked into his heavy zip-front boots. The wool mitts and toque, often carelessly tossed into his pocket, were donned with care today. He even put his hood up over the toque and wrapped his scarf around his neck, to cover the little piece of bare throat that he often left exposed.

The boy picked up the shovel from the landing and tried to open the back door. He met with immediate resistance. The snow was banked-in up to the knob. He was able to create by sheer force, a four inch opening, through which he reached his shovel. Probing his way through the crack with the shovel held sideways, he scratched a little path and sidestepped out. Elbowing the door closed, he stepped back six inches and began shoveling his way forward. He lifted scoop after scoop of snow above his chest, heav-

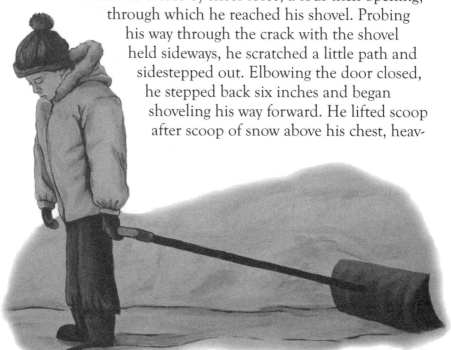

ing it over his shoulder onto the bank beside him. For an hour he repeated this motion as he shoveled from the back door, across the deck, onto the sidewalk and out to the street in front of his house. Then he shoveled the sidewalk that crossed in front of his house to his front door. He knew he still needed to shovel through the backyard out to the alley, where the garbage was picked up weekly. Garbage day wasn't for a couple days so he decided that could wait.

The boy and his friend met, feeling very proud that their work at home was complete. They were already tired but approached their day with confidence, plodding through waist-high snowbanks, in search of a potential customer. They had walked less than a block when the weight of the big steel shovels became too much for them. They knew they had to go back to their homes to select smaller spades. It was already ten in the morning. Quickly, they traded shovels at each of their homes and continued along the sloping street stopping at houses, knocking on doors, smiling and looking competent. They offered immediate snow removal to anyone they encountered. They heard many excuses. Some people had children of their own to remove snow. Others would do it themselves, later. One man decided he'd just leave it for this time because each time he shoveled, it just snowed again.

The boys progressed down the hill, no longer carrying their shovels over their shoulders in manly fashion. Instead, they dragged them behind, like toboggans. As the day became warmer, they wondered if they had overdressed. The boy lowered the hood of his coat. They never said it aloud but each boy was beginning to lose faith that there was work for them on this day.

Finally, they spotted the perfect house. There it was, at the bottom of the street. This yard was nicely kept. Silvery frost clung to the wire fence which was sturdily framed in clean white wood. The house, also white, had a cheerful yellow stripe all around it. It sat on a corner lot and it had a very long walk that went from the front street, along the side of the house through the backyard all the way to the garbage cans in the back alley. Where the snow had sifted down on its own, it had only amounted to about two and a half feet. Where it had accumulated because of obstruction, it was five or six feet deep. If anyone was at home today in the pretty little house, they were still there. The doors were snowed shut.

The boys struggled through waist high snow to the side door to offer their snow shoveling service. In answer to their knock, an old lady opened the inside door revealing her face, through the only corner of screen where snow had failed to cling. The boy realized that the lady didn't have a storm window on the door. He supposed she lived alone and really needed their help. When they asked if she needed them to clear her walk, she seemed overjoyed.

They began their work at the front street. As the sun warmed the snow it became more compact and heavy. They worked their way to the side of the house where there was no wind and the heat began to reflect off the siding. The boys had to clear the snow in layers, working down one foot at a time. It was like doing every section three times over. They began to perspire. They opened their coats. They grew thirsty.

To keep their spirits up, they talked about how much money the lady would likely pay them. They knew the job would take at least a couple of hours. They dared to hope that maybe they would get twenty-five or thirty cents between them. They could only imagine how neat it would be to get thirty cents. It would mean both of them could go to a movie on the weekend.

As lunch hour came and went, they kept shoveling past the house through the huge yard to the back alley. Finally, they each heaved their last shovel full of snow and took a moment to survey the job they had done. It was a good job. They felt pleasure.

They dragged their shovels back to the side door. The little old lady answered their knock with a big smile. From her window, she had been watching them work. She told them they had done a very professional job and that their parents could be very proud of them. She told them how surprised and grateful she was that they had taken time to help her. The boys enjoyed this praise more than they would have imagined. They were glad they had helped her. Again, they felt pleasure.

The old lady whispered that she had something for them. She slowly shuffled to the table in the middle of the room and picked two shiny red apples from a bowl. Then she turned toward the door and arduously covered the distance once again, this time opening the door and handing one to each boy. The boys were so hungry that their mouths filled with saliva at first bite. Then, it dawned on them, that this was all they were to receive for their work. Disappointment showed only in their posture.

They saw her stiff and crooked fingers reach into her apron and retrieve her change purse. Hopeful, they watched as she twisted the metal clasp, reached inside with her arthritic fingers and painstakingly withdrew a shiny silver coin. In the reflection of the sun, the coin appeared to be a quarter. When she assured them she had one for each of them, their hearts soared. That would be twenty-five cents each. That was absolutely amazing.

Thanking her, they turned to leave. As each boy felt the coin in his hand, it gradually became clear that he was holding a shiny silver nickel. They had spent the morning working extremely hard for an apple and a nickel each. They had done a good deed though. Part of that gave them pleasure. The other part left their shoulders and back aching without distraction. The shovels weighed more than they remembered. Their empty stomachs wept.

I think I know why my husband rarely enters into agreements without writing his expectations on paper for everyone involved to see. When I asked him what he learned from the snow removal experience he said, "Great rewards can come from good deeds or good deals. Always remember, there are apples, apple sauce and apple pie. It's just good for everyone to know, going in, which type of reward is expected."

Who's in Charge?

The boy and his brother grew up in a small Saskatchewan town, having moved there, in the early fifties. The boy's brother was six and a half years older than he was and their mother was careful not to push them together too often. She had arranged for them to share a bedroom so that they would know something of each other.

On the occasional Wednesday afternoon she would put the older brother in charge of the boy. Wednesday was what everyone referred to as a half-holiday in the small town. The stores were closed for the afternoon and that meant that the boy's father could take the boy's mother to the city to pick up stock for their store, have an early supper, enjoy each other's company and pretend it was a date.

On one such Wednesday afternoon, about an hour after their parents left, the doorbell rang. The boy and his brother had been hanging out peacefully but now they pushed each other aside to get to the door. As soon as the door was opened, the big brother's friends began coaxing him to join them in the fields behind the new houses. The boy's brother declined time and again gesturing toward the boy. The persuasion continued. The three friends came equipped with old boards and fence posts, several hammers, a bag of nails, rope and some very long poles. Their plan was to build a raft and

float it on the slough behind the new homes. Each of the three visitors wore the standard black rubber boots, accented by red rings around the tops and thick red soles. After much discussion the boy and his brother donned their own boots and set out with the others.

If the brother had noticed the size of the boy's little boots as they stood proudly beside his own, he might have felt a tiny spark of sympathy for the boy. Instead, his feelings were more of agitation at the responsibility of having to care for his much younger brother. As they left the house, he told the boy that he'd better sit quietly at the edge of the water. As the older brother, it was his responsibility to keep an eye on the boy. The big brother's idea of keeping an eye was just that. As long as he could see the boy, at whatever distance, he would have done his job.

At first, the boy watched with enthusiasm as the four bigger boys planned and hammered. He was actually in awe of their organizational ability. He thought they were brilliant at using the variety of wood each had contributed. He realized they would float the raft with one big boy at each corner. The poles would be used to propel the craft along.

Soon, they tested the vessel at the water's edge. Confident that it was water worthy they began to move farther from the shore. The boy knew he would need to jump on board at that very moment or sit alone on land for the rest of the afternoon. Without asking, he took a running leap toward the raft, barely catching the edge with the toes of his boots. He scrambled to the middle of the craft, sat down and made himself as small as he could, wrapping his arms tightly around his knees. For one minute, he allowed himself to think that the big boys were poling the raft along just for his enjoyment. It felt great!

It might have been an accident but one boy took a step toward him and suddenly the balance changed and water began to flow over the edge of the raft. The boy sprang to his feet as his backside became wet and instinctively moved toward his big brother, for protection. The older boys exchanged knowing glances. Everyone began to converge on the boy who now stood near one corner of the raft. Slowly the raft began to tip, submerging the corner where the boy and his brother stood. The small boy wore small boots and all around him were larger taller ones. As the water rose around the boots it became clear that it would fill the boy's boots first. Indeed it did.

Without saying a word, the boy's big brother had made it abundantly clear that a small boy didn't belong on the raft. In fact, once the boy's boots were full of water, he begged to go back to shore to dump them out. The older boys suggested they trade him a trip to shore for a promise to sit there quietly until they were done rafting. He willingly agreed.

The boy sat on shore and twisted his socks tightly to wring the water out. He rubbed his feet together in an attempt to warm them. The little crease between his eyebrows grew deeper as he tried to think of ways to set this grave injustice right. As upset as he was, he knew that the outing hadn't been a total loss because he had learned how to build a raft.

Who's in Charge?

I have seen the pain in my husband's eyes when he feels that everyone is against him. I know he is secretly waiting to set things right. When I asked him what he learned that day he said, "I learned that sometimes life encourages you to build your own raft, by giving you a boot full!"

Seasoned Campers

During one Saskatchewan summer, in the late fifties, the boy spent a great deal of time with a family of brothers. One day, two of the brothers invited the boy to go on an overnight adventure north of town in the rolling hills near the creek.

Planning for their camping trip was as much fun as going. It was decided that the brothers would bring their tent. Each boy would bring a sleeping bag. They would take tins of beans and spaghetti, spoons and a can opener. They would need matches to light a fire and water to drink. Flashlights would be a good idea. The rest of their needs would be met in the wild. The brothers' father took one look at their gear and offered to drive the campers the five miles to the creek. From there, it would be up to them to select a campsite from what nature offered.

The brothers were seasoned campers. After careful consideration of their environment, a location was chosen deep in one of the ravines that ran at right angles to the creek. This would provide shelter from the wind which was a constant prairie condition. The bushes and trees on each side of their spot would provide a little shade until the sun went down. The campers took time to dig a trench around the tent to divert water from their sleeping quarters, should they encounter rain.

Get a Bigger Wagon

They knew this was a precaution they didn't really need to take because rain was a rare visitor to the prairies.

Setting up camp filled the first couple of hours. A large portion of that time was spent gathering wood for the fire. Once the real chores were done, they explored their surroundings, looking for arrow heads and animal tracks. They made up stories about the history of the creek and fantasized about the adventurers that must have gone before them.

When someone mentioned being hungry, they built a fire. First they created a circular border out of rocks. They placed a large flat rock in the middle of the circle and formed a ring of twigs and small branches around the central rock. They peeled the labels from the tins of food, lit them on fire and dropped them quickly onto the ring to ignite it. As the fire began to burn they opened the precious tins of spaghetti and beans and placed them on the rock in the center of the heat. The smell of burning wood and steaming sweet tomato sauces mingled with the scent of hot tin and musty creek grasses. The wait for supper was wonderfully painful. When the beans began to bubble, they waited impatiently for the flames to die down before taking turns scooping from the tins. The first taste of food was instantly etched into each camper's memory. Hunger and the sense of satisfaction heightened their experience. They were invincible!

As the sun began to set, the boy and his friends decided to go into their tent and prepare for the sleep they knew would elude them. Flashlights swirled about on the canvas tent. At first, they laughed and talked.

Then, as the boys grew quieter the sounds of the night grew louder. One coyote howled and others yapped excitedly. An owl's wings flapped past the tent creating a swish of air. The branches brushed against their tent like claws trying to scratch through the canvas. The boys told their stories in a distracted manner, their words often dwindling into long pauses as they strained to listen and see into the dark. The tent grew silent but no one was sleeping.

They were still awake when the first crack of thunder shook the tent. They heard the first few plops of rain on the canvas above them. In minutes, the number of raindrops pelting them accelerated dramatically and the wind pushed relentlessly at the sides of their tent. The boys sat frozen as the pounding rain created so much noise that they could scarcely hear the explosions of thunder. Surely they were in the center of a battlefield!

Looking out, they realized that the little trench around their tent was useless. The water surged down the ravine, passing by them on each side, as it sliced through their trenches and ran into the creek below. Within an hour, the old tent allowed water to seep through the seams. Although the boys sat a few inches off the floor on their air mattresses, it would be only a matter of time before their sleeping bags would be soaking wet.

The boy and the brothers were afraid. They huddled together inside the tent shivering and cringing from the violent noise of the storm. There was nervous laughter as they talked about what they would tell their friends and estimated how long it would be until sunrise. After several hours and amid the chaotic cracking of thunder and howling of wind, one boy thought he heard a horn honk! Everyone thought he must be imagining things. Then, the three boys looked into each other's wide and hopeful eyes and allowed themselves to hear the horn. One of the brothers looked out and said he could see flashing lights a few ravines over. They were sure that whoever it was would be looking for them. Without a thought about their campsite, the boys set out with their flashlights waving. They ran anxiously toward the light, falling and sliding in the mud.

As the campers approached the lights, they realized that the drenched man standing with one arm through an open car window, blowing the horn and flashing the headlights, was the boy's father. What they didn't know, was that the boy's father had stood vigilant for the better part of an hour. The boy wanted to run to his dad and be folded inside his arms but instead, as the fear faded, he walked like a man up to his rescuer and calmly asked him why he was there. His father, allowing them their dignity, suggested that they might want to climb into the car and continue their camping in the basement of the boy's home.

I admired the boys in this story for testing themselves. In response to this story, I was sure my husband would say something about the relief of being rescued when things aren't going as smoothly as planned. When I asked him what he learned from this camping experience, all he said was, "Location, location, location!"

Just Under the Wire

In the small Saskatchewan town, spring was always a
welcome event. The weather provided that hot-cold
combination that made outdoor play comfortable. As
summer waited in the wings, families made a special ef-
fort to have one more skate or toboggan ride.

On one perfect spring day, the boy was sitting on
the step in front of his house, when his friend's father
pulled into the driveway. The friend leaned out of the
Ranchero window to offer the boy a lift to the creek to
go tobogganing. The boy disappeared inside his house
to get permission and reappeared wearing his warm
clothes and a huge smile. On the way to the creek, they
picked up another friend and the three boys talked
excitedly as the father sang along with the radio.

On this day, the creek was alive with boys and girls
enjoying spring. Most wore water repellant pants and
bulky coats and mitts. Enticed by the warm weather,
many kept their hats in their pockets, letting their heads
feel the wind for the first time in months.

After waiting in line for long periods between tobogganing turns, the boy and his friends grew impatient.
They had tobogganed often at the creek near town
and they knew that they were to stay in the designated
tobogganing areas. However, just this once, they decided
together, to break the rules and find a new slope.

After serious consideration of many alternatives, they selected a relatively rock-free hill, a quarter mile from the public site. There was a small pointed stone ahead and the occasional thin spot but other than that the slope was perfect. With no line-up, it wasn't long before they were careening freely down the hill.

The boy's larger friend was in first position. Behind him sat the boy and behind the boy sat their smaller friend. The driver shifted his weight to steer the toboggan past the pointed stone. What they didn't know, was that this was the visible peak, of a much larger rock. As they tried to miss it, the rock gashed the bottom of the wooden toboggan and tore a partial slat away from beneath the smaller boy's legs. The toboggan tilted as it glided against the side of the big rock, veered dramatically and began its descent in another direction. They were now bouncing down the rocky side of the hill. This, they knew, was not good.

Snow pushed through the hole, created by the missing slat and was piling up between the smaller boy's legs. It was obvious that this ride was out of their control as they bounced violently from rock to rock. They realized that they couldn't stop the toboggan with their hands and jumping off was not an option.

At the bottom of the hill, fencing off a four foot drop to the road, was a barbed wire fence. They were heading straight toward it! The larger friend, in front, let out a panicked wail.

Instinctively, the friend leaned back, pushing the boy flat. As the boy was crushed by his friend everything became dark for a second and then he felt himself slide back pushing their smaller friend completely off the toboggan. The bigger friend closed his eyes as they went under the barbed wire fence. They careened through the air over the four foot drop and flew safely over the much traveled road and the snow covered grasses that bordered the valley. Dazed, they landed upright on the frozen creek. As they reluctantly opened their eyes, they realized that they were uninjured. They began to laugh the tentative nervous laughs of those who feel they have just escaped with their lives. As relief swept over them, they relaxed. They began to wonder about their smaller friend.

An eerie creaking sound warned the boys that beneath them, everything was not as it should be. All around their toboggan the frozen creek began to sag, allowing water to seep onto the creek's surface. Then the ice that held them, gave away completely, and they sank slowly into the two feet of water that filled the creek. Initially unable to move, they soon reacted to the icy water that seeped through their clothes. Reflexes powered their quick jump onto more solid ice. From this more secure position they worked together to free the toboggan from the creek's grip. Soaking wet, shivering with cold and amazed at the experiences of the day, they looked earnestly around for cars that might be going back to town. Finally, a neighbor offered the miserable boys a lift.

The smaller friend had experienced quite a bump when he fell off the toboggan but he was dry and without cuts. He willingly pulled the toboggan for his wet and trembling friends. All three climbed gratefully into the offered transportation and rode quietly back to town. Their thoughts drifted toward warm blankets, hot cocoa and supper.

Later, sitting on the hot air vent in dry clothes and smelling the roast beef his mother was preparing for dinner, the boy felt safe and content. The adventures of the day began to transform themselves from terrifying, to tremendous, as he allowed the story to take shape in his mind. The tale would soon be ready for sharing with others.

I thought this experience might have taught my husband that rules are usually in place for good reasons. When I asked him what he learned on this day, he said, "You can plan all you want but during the rocky patches, you've just got to hold on and enjoy the ride. You can't always control where you're going to end up."

Justice

It was Christmas season in the nineteen fifties, in a small Saskatchewan town, and although the boy was young, he was remembering past Christmases. Today he daydreamed as he sat on the hot-air register to shake the morning chill. It was very dark outside but the street-lights illuminated the snowflakes as they drifted hypnotically past the window. In this half-light he felt peaceful and cozy. Usually, his mother sat near the heat with him but for now she was in the kitchen making coffee.

In a few days, it would be Christmas and the special day would begin early with lots of excitement. The family would open presents and his father would take some footage with their 8mm home movie camera. They would stay in their pajamas for hours. Tired from work, his father would nod off from time to time. Later in the afternoon, the house would fill with at least two dozen relatives.

The boy began thinking about his uncle. This uncle had a bothersome habit. The boy wasn't even sure why he felt so annoyed by him. Perhaps it was because this uncle always won at checkers. The boy was sure that no one else had noticed the uncle's behavior. The more he thought about it, the more he knew he needed to set things right. The boy decided that this Christmas he would have some fun at the uncle's expense.

Get a Bigger Wagon

Each December, the boy's mother would heap the wooden salad bowl with assorted Christmas nuts and place the silver crackers across the pile. His own family members would only treat themselves to a nut occasionally when they walked by the coffee table. This way the supply of expensive nuts would last for the whole season.

Each Christmas, as the two dozen relatives arrived and before their coats were placed in the closet, there was a whirlwind of greetings, hugging, and handshaking. In all of this activity no one seemed to notice what happened to the nuts. The boy knew exactly what happened. The uncle would remove his coat and take a minute to talk to each of the relatives and then as the visiting ensued, he would pick up the bowl of Christmas nuts, find the most comfortable chair, sit down and center the bowl on his lap. He would crack nut after nut, dropping the shells into the bowl, retrieving the edible part and chewing greedily, with Christmas happening all around him. The boy found this behavior unacceptable!

This year would be different. In preparation for his plan the boy took a handful of walnuts to his room each day. He worked with precision to crack the nuts into perfect halves. When he failed to split them exactly in two, the shells were thrown away. When they split perfectly, he glued the hollow walnuts together with absolutely nothing but air inside. As the week went on, the supply of hollow nuts grew and on Christmas afternoon, before the company arrived, the boy mixed his stash of special nuts in with the others. He made sure there were enough full nuts in the bowl to give the uncle little reason to suspect tampering. The boy smiled as he anticipated the unfolding of his scheme.

The guests arrived and, as usual during the visiting, no one noticed the uncle pick up the bowl and place it on his lap. The boy sat nonchalantly in a big arm chair across the room and watched as the uncle cracked one nut and then another. Always, the shells fell into the bowl. Often, he had to retrieve the edible part from amid the bits of shell and whole nuts.

Then it happened! The uncle squeezed the cracker with his usual exceptional strength and the force exploded a hollow nut. He grimaced as he caught his finger between the arms of the cracker as it closed completely on nothing but shell and air. The uncle looked through the debris in the bowl to see where the edible part might have fallen. He couldn't find a shelled nut to eat. Puzzled, he prepared to crack another one. Again, the uncle picked a hollow nut. The look of bewilderment on his face only lasted a minute because the next nut was full. He shrugged the whole incident off. For the better part of an hour, the boy sat enjoying the culmination of his plan. The uncle opened full nuts, then hollow nuts, followed by more full nuts and then a hollow one. He appeared puzzled and fittingly frustrated. When the guests were called to dinner, the uncle and the boy stood like all the others, walked to the table and kept their respective secrets to themselves.

Get a Bigger Wagon

I have seen my husband's face when he is pleased with a perfectly planned scheme. I knew this moment in his life had given him a sense of being able to control a situation. No one needed to know except him, that justice had occurred. When I asked him what he learned from this incident he said, "Many businesses are like hollow nuts. They look like they should on the outside but there isn't much inside." I guess once you have made hollow nuts you are more aware of what others are offering you.

Harvest

One summer in the late fifties, in a small Saskatch-ewan town, a boy made friends with a whole family of brothers. There were four brothers in the family and, like the boy, they were very good at thinking of creative ways to spend their time. Once a week, two or more of the brothers would spend the night in their backyard in the old musty tent.

The brothers had a very unique backyard. It was enormous and was bordered on one side by their grand-mother's equally large yard. Alleys bordered the back and remaining side. Perpendicular to these alleys were several smaller yards. Every one of these had a garden. When the brothers spent the night in the backyard, there were at least six gardens within easy picking dis-tance of their tent.

Another good thing about the yard was that it was basically free of landscaping. This meant that the boys could build miles of roadway and create whole towns in the black dirt. There was serious excavating going on at all times.

The boy enjoyed every minute he spent in the broth-ers' backyard. Sometimes, in preparation for a visit, he and the brothers would collect Popsicle sticks for days. There were always many on the ground near the corner store and a trail of them could be followed all the way to

the swimming pool. Popsicle sticks could be stuck into the dirt or stacked log cabin style, to create wonderful forts for lead soldiers to hide behind.

Small skirmishes and major battles were staged in the brothers' backyard. Sometimes, there were serious attacks on these forts resulting in complete destruction. This occurred when a stream of lighter fluid was trickled towards the forts and ignited from a safe distance. Such complex battle maneuvers were always supported by the nearby water hose, just in case a prairie wind should catch the flames and fan things out of control.

Usually, during one of these great games, someone would suggest that the boy should sleep over so that the great adventures could continue. The boy would bike to his home to fetch his brother's sleeping bag, inform his mother and be back to the yard in minutes. Sometimes, as dusk swept over the yard, they built a fire and roasted wieners. Often, they nibbled on crabapples from the many trees that lined the huge yard.

The neighbors always knew when the boys slept outside. There was laughing, shouting and occasional flashlight beams on their windows. When things did quiet down, the neighbors would go to sleep. Then, the boys would creep stealthily to the alleys, climb the fences and pick carrots and potatoes from the forbidden gardens. The boy's favorite garden treat would have been peas, but they were too hard to pick in the dark.

The day after each sleepover, the neighbors would notice missing produce, phone the brothers' mother and report the damages. They hadn't seen the raiding but it was suggested that if the boys were doing it, they should stop!

Get a Bigger Wagon

One night, the brothers and the boy talked quietly inside the tent. The neighbors didn't hear them planning. They needed to find a way to have these late night adventures without their neighbors' knowledge. After posing many ideas, a plan evolved. This night, they would carefully dig around the plants, gently lift them out, harvest the carrots and potatoes and replant the foliage. They knew that flimsy carrot tops could only be replanted properly if a portion of the carrot was left to support the plant. This would require patiently snapping off the slim ends for themselves, while leaving some roots. The procedure would take longer but if they started later, allowing everyone in the neighborhood to fall soundly asleep, it could work!

The escapade was exciting and went exactly as planned. Back in the tent they shared deliciously sweet carrots seasoned with a bit of dirt. The taste would remain in their minds forever! Potatoes, juicy and starchy, were made palatable by the sense of adventure the group experienced from foraging for food. They were one with every hunter-gatherer that ever walked the earth.

As the sun came up and warmed the musty tent, the wonderful smell of old canvas, dirt and sweat comforted them and they reluctantly gave in to sleep. There were no phone calls that day because there was no evidence of garden raiding. When they took off their shoes though, there was a tell-tale dirt smudge between each toe on each foot. No one was there to notice.

Each time the brothers and the boy camped out in the yard, they repeated the new raiding procedure.

August turned into September, camping ended and
school resumed. In the gardens at the back of the yards,
bordering the brothers' home, some plants simply
wilted to a slow and premature death, while others re-
rooted and remained healthy looking on top. The raids
had been spaced over a few weeks so the plants that
died, did so at intervals. No one was suspicious. The
wilting was blamed on some rare root disease.

As harvest began, the neighbors wondered about
the lack of vegetables beneath such healthy foliage. They
didn't seem to suspect that the garden pests were really
the backyard campers. No one seemed to notice that the
blight only occurred in the gardens that bordered the
brothers' home. As with so many of life's unexplained
situations, there never was a recurrence of that particular pest and soon enough it was forgotten.

*I thought my husband would tell me about the joy of execut-
ing a perfect plan, in answer to my usual question about what
he had learned. Instead, he answered, "I learned to look beneath
the surface. Companies and people need strong roots. You have to
watch for early signs of wilting."*

Dream Destroyed

For many months, the boy had anticipated owning the shiny new three-speed bicycle. He had earned it by steadfastly collecting bottles and doing odd jobs. The counting, calculating and predicting had filled his free time. At last, he knew the satisfaction of having accomplished the goal he had set for himself.

On this fall day, he finished his after-school jobs at his father's store and left through the back door to get his cherished bike. He felt a wave of excitement as he threw his leg over the bar and settled onto the seat. He rode in the back allies, through ditches and parks, and then looped back to the main street of the little prairie town. He navigated this street more cautiously, as he approached the angle parking spots that edged the downtown businesses. All too often, drivers backed into the main street, concentrating only on their next destination. A small cyclist could easily go unnoticed.

He rode aimlessly down graveled side streets, on cement sidewalks, across cracked pavement and over the town's only remaining boardwalk. He enjoyed the sound of his wheels on the various surfaces. There was swishing, snapping, scratching and then the hollow thumping sound of his wheels crossing the well-worn wooden boards. He was sure he could identify these surfaces with his eyes shut. He practiced changing the gears of his bicycle until he could do it almost seamlessly.

From the alley behind the post office, he could see his good friend walking toward him. This friend, also worked after-school, and was finished for the day. The boy could hardly wait to show his friend the new three-speed bicycle. He hailed him with a wave.

Like a salesman, the boy detailed the features of his new bike. He wasn't surprised when the friend asked for a ride home. He invited the friend to hop onto the bar in front of him. The journey began, as the boy put the bike in low gear, demonstrating how easy it was to gain momentum, in spite of the extra weight of a passenger. This was the joy of owning a three-speed bike. Build-ing up speed, the boy eased his machine into second gear and both little faces opened into huge smiles. As the bike accelerated, they felt the pure pleasure of the moment.

Then, without warning, the rear end of the bicycle flipped up in a reverse wheel-stand and catapulted the boy into the air, over the friend's head and on for sev-eral bike lengths. Even when he landed on the cindered alley, his body continued to be propelled along the jagged surface for several feet. Neither victim knew what had caused this sudden calamity. The boy slowly became aware of the painful heat on his cheeks and hands. This awareness was followed by a wave of anxiety about the probable damage to his bicycle.

The boy slowly pulled his body to a standing position and stumbled toward his bike. His friend was moaning and squirming on the ground, holding his foot with one hand and his ankle with the other. The spokes, missing from the bicycle's front wheel, provided evidence that his passenger had accidentally caught his foot.

As the boy absorbed the damage to his bicycle, he angrily stamped his foot and swung both arms downward. He realized that his friend was pointing at him, trying to tell him something about the condition of his face. The boy looked down at his burning hands and was sickened by the sight of his raw and bleeding palms. The skin had been grated away by the sharp and unforgiving cinders. The boy and his friend stared into each other's faces with total disbelief. His friend offered to move the bike from the alley, to the approach behind a nearby garage. The boy nodded with gratitude and hurriedly turned toward his father's store. In the time it took to reach the store, the searing pain screamed from his cheeks and hands and the boy burst into the store shouting for his father.

As if choreographed and filmed in slow motion, the customers turned their heads all at once toward the injured boy. It was impossible to know what had happened to him because the bleeding was so diffused. The cinders had peeled the top layer of skin from one smooth round cheek and scraped the chin, eyebrow and lips, thus far unscarred by the boy's many adventures. The customers' faces grimaced as they observed the bleeding child. His father, a gentle man, often bothered by the sight of blood, led him stoically to the back of the store, speaking softly as he began to assess the damage.

While the father rinsed and medicated the wounds, the boy tried to convince him to retrieve the bike. The injuries, the boy was sure, could wait. His father knew the jagged cinders had done a great deal of damage to his son's face and it needed to be tended to, carefully. The bike, he was sure, could wait.

The garage, behind which the bike was left, belonged to a prominent, wealthy, and very old citizen of the little town. At precisely the same time as the boy was getting his face repaired, the elderly man was leaving his home through the back door, entering his garage from the yard door and getting into his car. He didn't hear the crunch or feel the bump as he backed his sturdy nineteen forty-nine Ford sedan, over the boy's shiny three-speed bicycle. He drove toward the country-side, oblivious to the destruction he had left behind.

When the boy and his father arrived at the garage and took in the sight, their hearts sank. The front wheel of the bike was crushed beyond recognition. The boy's face and hands hurt even more as his spirit staggered under the weight of the realization that he would have to buy a new front wheel.

He spent the evening quiet and sad. He thought about his options. He knew the old man was wealthy. Maybe he would want to repair the bicycle. He would visit the man, the next day.

In the morning, the boy rang the old man's door-bell. He began by inquiring as to the well being of the man's car. The old man seemed confused, so the boy told him the whole story about how the bike was left on the approach after the accident, because he had serious injuries that needed to be tended to. He told the old man, that he understood how easy it would be to get into the car, having entered the garage from the yard side, and just back out over a bicycle, that wasn't supposed to be there. The boy stopped talking and looked deep into the old man's eyes, for a sign of sympathy or remorse. The old man looked down at the little bandaged face, with the swollen eye and scabby lips, and remained expressionless. The old man gruffly assured the boy that he would certainly remember running over a bicycle, if he had done such a thing, and he certainly had not. The boy left the house feeling strangely embarrassed about ever having hoped for help from the old man. He would simply solve this problem on his own.

Once more, the boy began to get estimates, to pick and haul bottles, to keep records and count days. His dad offered him a few extra hours at the store and when the boy was nearing the amount he needed for the new wheel, it was his dad, who gave him the last few dollars.

After every major disappointment in our lives, my husband has been quiet for a time, and then bounced back with resilience. Sometimes, these introspective moods would last for a couple of days and sometimes for a few hours. Always, they resulted in a plan.

When I asked my husband what he learned from this experience, he replied, "Well, it confirmed the wisdom of my mom's constant reminder that riding double causes trouble. However, I prefer to look at this series of events as one more first for me. I was the first kid in my town to have a three-speed bicycle and on this day, I became the first kid in town to have a unicycle!"

Moving Out

It was one of those days in summer when you feel so warm and relaxed that everything is less urgent. The boy was at home with his brother who was watching over him while his parents were in the nearby city, an hour or so away. The brother was six and a half years older than the boy so they had little in common. During the time they spent together on this day, the brother polished his cadet boots, did homework and talked on the phone. The boy shadowed his brother's every move, waiting for him to fulfill his promise to play a game of checkers, when the tasks were done.

The whole problem started with a phone call in the late afternoon. The big brother's friends wanted him to come to the ball game. There was a short exchange of refusals and persuasions and then the brother checked his watch, did a few mental calculations and gave in to the offer. He figured that by the time their parents ate a meal in the city and drove home it would be about eight-thirty in the evening. The ball game would be over a few minutes after eight. It would be close, but it could work!

The boy begged his brother to let him attend the game. The baseball games were always exciting and he could already taste the hotdogs. The brother impatiently explained that his friends wouldn't want some little kid hanging around the ball field with them. Then he warned the boy that he should stay in the house, watch television and not mention this to his parents or else. He didn't elaborate on the, or else, but the boy understood.

The brother's friends arrived to pick him up and the boy found himself alone in the house wondering how he could get his brother in trouble, without actually telling on him. It needed to be sort of an accident. As he sat, alone, he became more and more angry. They hadn't even played the promised checker game. He thought he probably hated his brother.

Then, it came to him! He would move out of their bedroom and into his parent's room. He would rather live there anyway. They, of course, would ask him what was wrong. He couldn't be blamed if his parents pried it out of him.

The boy didn't own much, but when you really mean to move everything, even a modest collection creates a large pile. He emptied the drawers that were his and he reverently placed these drawers on his parent's bed. He gathered every sock, shirt and piece of underwear as well as every book, board game and shoe and placed it all in or near the drawers. He moved his clock, his radio and his lamp as well as the hanging clothes from the closet. The pile on their bed was enormous. They would definitely notice!

At ten minutes after eight in the evening, the big brother entered the house calling to the boy. The brother looked through the kitchen to the living room and found no one. He checked the bathroom and the basement. His heart beat faster as he realized the boy must have left the house. His parents would be back in minutes! He called to the boy again and then again. Finally, a muffled response from the end of the hall provided him with a sense of relief.

The big brother followed the sound to his parent's room, entered and was genuinely dismayed to find the enormous pile of stuff on their bed. His face contorted into sheer panic. There was so little time until his parents would be home. He went into unprecedented negotiation mode. He promised to take the boy on an outing anywhere he wanted to go. He, of course, would fulfill his promise to play checkers with the boy. The boy could have anything else he wanted but for now they should work together to put the bedrooms right. As he spoke, he hastily piled things onto the boy's outstretched arms and gathered huge loads himself. As the last sock was returned to the dresser drawers and the dresser drawers themselves were put back in place, their mom and dad entered the house chatting cheerfully, and announced their arrival.

That evening just before bed, the two brothers played checkers together and the parents looked on fondly, feeling assured that the boys were becoming really good friends. For the parents, this was the perfect end to a perfect day.

I know my husband has often taken drastic action when he feels that things are out of his control and he needs to be heard. When I asked him what he learned during this experience he thought for a moment and then he said, "An urgent timetable will always increase the speed of the negotiations and the size of the settlement."

Close Call

One spring day in the small Saskatchewan town, the boy sat in school with his hands under his chin and his eyes fixed on the view outside the window. A violent storm had raged through the town the previous night. Now, the sun shone brightly on the puddles of melted snow and light bounced toward his eyes. Everywhere, there was evidence of the chaos caused by the storm. Broken branches, shingles, chunks of paper and other debris had been plastered to the school fence during the night. The boy longed to investigate the town to see what damages might have occurred.

That day he enjoyed his walk home for lunch. The sheltered areas were actually warm. It was easy to believe that summer was near, yet the windy places were a harsh reminder that winter was still hovering. He wore blue jeans, a plaid shirt, a cardigan and a Melton-cloth jacket which he zipped and un-zipped depending on the shelter available. On his feet he wore his new black canvas boot-style runners with the white rubber toes. It was the first day of walking without his heavy winter boots and he was aware of how light his feet felt. For no particular reason, the boy broke into a run, feeling like he could almost fly. He burst into the door of his home, inhaled deeply and realized his mom had made macaroni with cheese and tomatoes. He was starving.

Get a Bigger Wagon

After lunch, he walked reluctantly in the direction of the school. Eventually, he couldn't resist the need to explore. He snuck down the back alley toward the fields. As he approached the town's enclosed baseball stadium, he realized that during the storm, some of the tall wooden walls had crashed down around the bleachers. This was an excellent opportunity for climbing.

For the boy, time stood still, while he bounced up and down on the boards, creating a squeaking sound. Then, flat on his back on the downed fence, he watched the clouds change shapes and absorbed the warmth of the boards. Standing up, he began to spring from board to bouncy board, propelled through the air between jumps, like a circus performer.

It was after one of these leaps that the unthinkable happened. He heard the terrible squeal of metal puncturing rubber and when he looked down, the sheer horror of what had happened took a moment to sink in. There, protruding from the center of the toe of his running shoe was about five inches of an eight inch spike. He had landed on this nail and was now impaled upon it and firmly attached to the boards. He waited for the pain. He had heard that shock often delayed the true agony of injury. He thought he should feel some discomfort, though.

He carefully secured his balance on the uninjured foot and inch by inch lifted the punctured foot off of the nail. There was a long drawn out screech as the rubber and canvas shoe was dragged back up the spike. He immediately unlaced his shoe, took it off and discovered a hole in his sock, right between his big toe and the one beside it. He couldn't believe his good luck! He had made a big mistake. He knew he shouldn't jump on lumber without checking for nails. Then, having jumped on a nail, he was blessed that it had entered right between his toes. It was such a surprising event that he knew none of his friends would believe him. He would have to keep the sock and the shoe forever.

With these thoughts he began his walk toward home. Historically, whenever he skipped school, he hid in a neighbor's garage until the high school near his home was dismissed. When the bell rang, he would wait another ten minutes to allow for the time it usually took to walk home from his elementary school. This way his escapades went undiscovered. To arrive undetected at this garage, he usually cut through the deep drainage ditches that bordered the streets near the high school. Feeling cold and tired after the incident with the nail, he anticipated the shelter the garage could provide from the spring wind.

Get a Bigger Wagon

He walked down the alley, over the culverts and toward the ditch. He stepped confidently onto the slopping side and began his descent. He carefully took two test steps onto the crusted snow that filled the ditch. Feeling that the surface would hold him, he moved forward another two steps and plunged abruptly into the depths of the water below. Stunned, he realized that he was up to his armpits in frigid slush! This time the pain was immediate. It felt as if someone was squeezing his chest and poking pins into his fingers and toes. He was unable to breathe! He was freezing.

It seemed to the boy that it took forever to free himself from the ditch. In reality, he made an immediate escape, running without hesitation to the shelter of the garage where he knew he had to wait until the high school bell rang. The garage provided welcome protection from the chilly wind but he was still cold and wet. Safe in the garage, he thought for the first time about the fact that he could have drowned in the ditch.

He knew if he could wait until the correct time to arrive home, he could tell his mom about the accident as if it had happened on his walk from school. She would be very sympathetic as she wrapped him in blankets. He imagined she would make him hot chocolate. Maybe she would offer him a cookie. Certainly there would be hugs. He just had to make this work!

His lips were feeling numb. Steam drifted from his mouth and his nose. He began to shake uncontrollably. His chin trembled and that made his round cheeks vibrate. He still had at least an hour to wait until the bell would ring. For the first time there was a glimmer of worry in his wide green eyes. The Melton-cloth coat smelled like a wet cat. He took off his mitts and realized his finger nails were purple. His toque was still dry so he put it on his hands. This warmed his hands but left his head uncomfortably cold. As he bounced up and down to warm himself he realized he even had to go to the bathroom. Things weren't going very well.

He weighed the horrible discomfort of this moment against the pain he would experience if his mom learned that he had skipped school again. As he shivered, he allowed himself to consider the idea that his mom might not even be at home. Maybe she had gone shopping or to a neighbor's house for tea. Maybe he was suffering needlessly. The pain was growing greater and he realized he would have to take the gamble. He ran toward the warmth of his house, hoping, even praying, that his mom, just this once, might be out.

As he opened the door to his warm home, his mother stood at the top of the three stairs leading to the kitchen. It was like a movie running in fast forward. She pelted him with questions but he heard only fragments. In the time it took him to climb the three steps he had heard, "too early, why home, what thinking and why wet," and then she took a firm hold on his ear and ushered him into the bathroom. Here she ran him a tub, told him to get in and warm up and promised him an unforgettable conclusion to his adventuring!

I am surprised that my husband's sense of adventure remained intact after such a day. I thought he would tell me this story taught him that even the best ideas can fail to work out. When I asked my husband what he learned that day, all he said was, "One, two, three strikes, you're out...of luck, that is!"

Out of Control

It was spring in the small Saskatchewan town. The winter had provided bountiful gifts of snow, that once melted, had been sipped up swiftly by the parched prairie clay. The boy's muddy rubber boots stood proudly on the step like soldiers after the battle. The boy wore his high-top runners and rode his bicycle in large circles on the dry road, always aware of oncoming cars.

The boy had many good friends and on lazy Saturdays he usually spent time with some of them. He knew a family of four brothers, all close to his own age, who always had good ideas. On this spring Saturday, the boy was happy to see two of these brothers riding toward him. The brothers followed the boy as he made circular patterns on the road. One of them suggested taking a ride to the creek. He was sure the water would be deeper than usual because of the melted snow. They agreed to ride their bicycles, wear their rubber boots and pack food and water. In a matter of minutes, they were pedaling down the highway to their next adventure.

After a long ride, the brothers and the boy arrived at the top of the valley. They left their bikes near the road and began to meander through the hills, searching for something to investigate. As they descended the hills to the base of the valley, they realized that the creek, was indeed, much wider than usual. They spent time throwing rocks, mentally measuring the distance covered and the size of the splash. Looking for frogs, they stumbled upon an old skull, likely from a buffalo. They idled the moments away, soaking up the sun and the bitter smells of spring.

Then, like many times before, someone had an idea. It began with one boy suggesting that they play firemen. Without planning, another boy set fire to a patch of last year's dead thistles and grasses. Someone suggested letting it get a little bigger. It formed a six foot square with the creek on one side. Then as if on cue, three pairs of rubber boots began stomping the fire out. Each boy took a side, leaving the creek to take care of the fourth. The flames licked at their feet just enough to cause excitement. By the time they had extinguished the fire, the little firemen were intoxicated with their own power.

As one boy suggested they do it again, another lit a match. For a couple of hours, the brothers and the boy repeated the pattern by lighting the grass, letting the flame grow a little larger, conquering it and feeling very excited. They were having so much fun that not one of them noticed the wind beginning to participate in their game.

Then, the unthinkable happened. The fire was respectably large and the boys began to stomp it out, working their way toward the creek as they had done repeatedly, all day. This time, as each boy worked along his edge, one of the brothers noticed that the fire was traveling beyond him. His frantic stomping wasn't working and the strong wind he felt in his face, explained why. It was as if the wind was having a race with the flames.

The brothers and the boy joined forces on one side of the fire, against the wind. They ran back and forth stomping, shouting ideas and feeling sick inside. Each of them repeatedly filled a boot with water and poured it on the flames. When that failed, they tried pouring water on the grass ahead of the fire in an attempt to stop its progress. The possible outcome of their game was too awful to think about.

Then, as if one of their ancestors had reached down from the sky to help out, the fire began to slow. The boys ran ahead and gradually realized that they might have an opportunity to set things right. Across the path of the fire and perpendicular to the creek, there was a barbed wire fence. On each side of this fence was a dirt cow-path. Without verbalizing a plan, the boys placed themselves beyond the fence and paths. They waited for the fire to try to jump the obstruction. Voracious little tongues of flame tried to consume the grass here and there, beyond the barrier. The boys faced the small flames and vanquished them, one at a time. Then it was over. They kept watch like sentries for over an hour after the last determined spark leapt the paths. Confident that they had won, they slumped onto the ground in complete exhaustion and began admitting to each other that they had almost caused a disaster.

As they walked slowly up the hills toward the road to retrieve their bikes, one brother suggested that they make some sort of promise to each other. They ceremoniously dug a hole, knelt beside it, buried the matches and pledged never again to light fires. They marked the spot with a carefully built cairn to remind themselves, at every visit to the creek, of this near catastrophe. As they rode home in silence, the brothers and the boy reviewed the day somberly.

Upon arriving home, the boy placed his rubber boots back on the front steps, where they stood taller and wiser than before. After that day, the boys never spoke about the fire, to each other or to anyone else. Their secret would be kept forever.

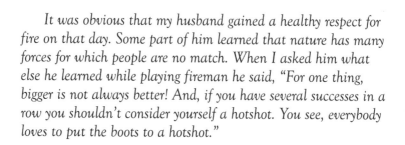

It was obvious that my husband gained a healthy respect for fire on that day. Some part of him learned that nature has many forces for which people are no match. When I asked him what else he learned while playing fireman he said, "For one thing, bigger is not always better! And, if you have several successes in a row you shouldn't consider yourself a hotshot. You see, everybody loves to put the boots to a hotshot."

The Fist Fight

In the mid-fifties, in a small Saskatchewan town, the boy moved with his family to a new neighborhood where they had built a cozy little bungalow. The picture window in their living room looked directly across the road to the high school's football field. Each winter, in the schoolyard, a rectangular sheet of ice, edged with boards about a foot high, would magically appear and skating and hockey games would ensue. By day, the school custodian ensured that the rink was clean for scheduled activities. On weekends and at night, it was available for use by anyone who was willing to scrape the snow from its surface.

One day, a few of the boys in the neighborhood were playing a shorthanded game of hockey, after clearing the snow off the ice. One of the players, a neighbor who lived two doors south of the boy, was bigger than the rest but not as agile. He had trouble skating while maneuvering the wide snow scraper, sometimes tripping on the very blade he pushed. His mood grew darker as the ice grew clearer.

When the game started, the large neighbor kid began a series of irritating attacks on the boy, who was happily tending the net. Like the others, the boy wore no protective equipment. Everyone obeyed the rules and kept their sticks on the ice except the big kid. He shot the puck time after time at the goal, frequently

ushering the puck right into the net, after distracting the boy by slashing at him with his stick.

In pain, and angered by this treatment, the boy warned his attacker several times to stop. Eventually, having had enough, he charged from the net, straight toward the substantially larger boy. Facing him, the boy wrapped his right leg around the back of his assailant's knees, forcefully jerking them forward. The big kid buckled and fell flat on his back. The little goalie straddled him, fists clenched and ready.

Just as the boy was about to pummel the big kid's chest, he felt himself being lifted by the hood of his parka. The cold metal zipper cut into the front of his throat and his scarf slipped up over his face. Grabbing for his scarf, he squirmed back and forth, in an attempt to get a look at his captor.

The man held the boy in pretty much the same way as a flying hawk clutches a mouse. Spinning the boy around to face him, the man announced that he had seen the whole thing and went on about how the boy should know better than to attack his friends. He hauled the boy through the ditch, over the road and deposited him roughly on his mother's door step. She listened to the accusatory speech, thanked him for returning her son and mentioned that there were often many interpretations of a story. She might have whispered something about the importance of letting boys work out their own differences. Then she ushered the boy inside to hear his version of the story. She listened calmly, made little of the whole situation and assured him that an opportunity would eventually present itself for working things out in private.

Get a Bigger Wagon

Even though the large neighbor kid lived only two doors away from the boy, there was never a time that winter, when the two played alone. Always, there were other children from the neighborhood to diffuse the tension that remained between them.

One day in summer, as the boy was shooting marbles on the sidewalk, the big neighbor kid approached him. At first, they appeared to be talking nicely on the street in front of the boy's house. Then their voices grew louder and louder and finally, the big kid shoved the boy with both hands. The boy shoved back and the fight was on. The noise brought the boy's mother out of the house and she told them that the time had come to go into the backyard, close the gate and figure things out.

The gate was closed, the mother returned to the house and the rivals stood facing each other, wondering what to do next. To gain focus, the boy thought back to the night on the ice in the schoolyard and he once again felt angry! He decided to show the big guy that he was not going to be pushed or hit by him with a hockey stick ever again. He made a fist by tucking his thumb into his four curled fingers. He took aim and directed every ounce of strength he had toward the bigger boy's jaw. Both boys dropped to their knees howling, then sprang to their feet hopping in anguish.

At the moment of impact, the boy felt the joints of his thumb collide together like cars in a pileup. He thought they might have actually slid inside one another and he realized the tucking of his thumb into his curled fingers was a grave mistake. The pain traveled like a sharp blade right up to his wrist and he felt hot tears rolling down his face. The big kid winced from the pain in his jaw and the sting caused by his teeth piercing the side of his tongue. The howling and hopping continued until the boy, realizing how silly they looked, fell onto the ground, laughing uncontrollably. The neighbor kid also began to smile and then to laugh. When the laughing subsided, there was more rubbing of injuries, a little complaining and more airing of grievances.

Soon someone had an idea for an adventure they could have that very afternoon. When the boy's mother looked out of the window, the two were walking side by side out of the yard.

I was sure my husband would tell me that what he learned from the interfering neighbor was that one should gather all the facts before drawing a conclusion. When I asked him what he learned from this incident, he smiled at me and said, "I learned I was going to be a lover, not a fighter." Then, he told me the incident taught him most problems are best solved privately between those directly involved.

The Payback

It was one of those sunny summer Sundays that beckons to people of all ages. As the boy's parents sipped their morning coffee on the patio they were lulled into summer's arms by the lazy swishing sound of the water sprinklers. Helpless, they allowed themselves to be seduced into a rare moment of summer spontaneity. Cups left behind, they quickly arranged for the boy's older brother to watch over him and they made a hasty retreat down the driveway into the awaiting day. They were off to the city and they weren't sure when they'd be back. They directed their sons to have the sweet and sour ribs in the fridge for supper. As their mother blew them kisses from the open window of the car, the puzzled boys stood beside each other, waving mechanically. After a sustained pause, they turned and went indoors.

The boy loved to tinker. In the family basement, he busied himself with the miniature pool table he had built from scraps of lumber. The little table was as level as he could make it. Green felt covered the solid one inch plywood that formed the base. A frame about one and a half inches high, made from very thin wood, held the felt securely in place. Inside this frame were pieces of foam, covered in strips of first-aid adhesive tape. This provided perfect banks. A series of holes drilled together allowed for the removal of a piece of the plywood base

Get a Bigger Wagon

at each of the four corners, creating pockets. Dowelling,
measuring three-eighths of an inch in diameter, made
a perfect pool cue for the half-inch marbles he used to
make his shots. On this little table, he and his friends
learned the principles of playing pool.

The big brother polished his boots and the buttons
on his cadet uniform. Then he went to the back deck
to do some assigned reading. Sometime before lunch
the doorbell rang. The boy and his brother heard it
and approached from two directions. They noticed a
jet black Mercury four-door hardtop in the driveway. It
sat shiny and proud in the sunlight, windows down and
radio blaring. The boy recognized his brother's friends.
They were planning to go to the lake and wanted the
brother to go too. The boy's brother protested. He was
in charge of the boy and couldn't leave home. The
persuasion was followed by a good rebuttal which was
followed by another persuasion and so it continued, like
a table tennis game, punctuated with dramatic gestures.

The boy suddenly remembered that the brother owed
him the outing of his choice because of a past grievance.
He burst into the conversation excitedly informing everyone that he chose this outing as his payback. His brother
could go to the lake. They would all go to the lake! The
big brother's expression smoothly changed from an "in
your dreams" roll of his eyes, to a "well, maybe you've
got something there" smile, and the simple solution
became clear. The decision had been made.

The big brother slid into the front seat. The boy
rode in the back, behind the driver and across the seat
from the other friend. The windows were down and the

boys draped their arms casually on the doors, elbows slightly through the open windows, shirt sleeves billowing in the wind. They wore sunglasses and played the music too loud. Conversation was impossible and unnecessary. Each boy had his own personal thoughts. From behind the car, it would have been easy to see that one passenger could barely reach the open window. One head was barely visible over the rear seat. Still, the boy was sure he looked just like the older guys.

The trip to the lake was uneventful. Summer's warm winds whistled and roared through the open windows making the Hit-Parade barely audible. As they pulled onto the winding bumpy road that led to the lake, one boy suggested that they park alongside the bushes in a slightly shaded area and take a moment to have a beer. The driver found a spot and pulled over. He removed the keys from the ignition, got out of the car and went to the trunk. He quickly returned to the vehicle with a box of beer. The driver opened one and passed it to his friend in the back. Then, he gave one to the boy's brother. He casually opened his own and took a mouthfull. The driver held the beer in his mouth for a long time, as if he was savoring it.

The older boys drank and talked and then to the young boy's amazement his brother reached back and offered him a taste! In slow motion, he saw himself extend his hand to take the brown glass bottle from his big brother. The boy smiled with delight at this acknowledgement. He took a long sustained gulp. He thought this might be the coolest thing he had ever done. Then, he began to actually taste, the vile sour stuff. He knew this was the worst thing he had ever consumed. He wiped his mouth off on his arm, gave the bottle back to his brother and thanked him offhandedly.

When the beer was gone, the boys went for a walk down by the lake. They pointed out familiar cabins and talked about their owners. Each of them knew someone with a cabin at this lake. They stopped at the little store for some chips and pop. It became clear that not much was happening at the lake on this day, so they went back to the car to head for home.

The drive back started out just like the drive to the lake. The boys should have been home long before their parents. The radio tunes beat on and the open windows allowed the whirling winds to roar past and through the car, enabling each passenger to become lost in his own thoughts.

Then the driver excitedly announced that just ahead, there was a car full of girls wearing ponytails. The driver could see that the prairie highway was clear for miles so he pulled out and sped up beside them. The girls' windows were down and before long they were leaning out, waving and talking excitedly to the older boys. The young boy hoped the driver was keeping an eye out for on-coming cars because the two vehicles were beside each other, traveling at exactly the same speed.

The girls shouted an invitation to a party. When the boy's brother indicated he had to take his little brother home, they smiled fondly at the small boy and gestured that everyone could come. That seemed like a great idea so the older boys pulled behind the girls and followed them into town.

The Payback

To the boy's amazement they all went to the party. It was one of those parties where you forget your obligations. There were girls to dance with and interesting foods to eat. The boy sat quietly, watching everything that went on around him. He would have been content to sit there for hours. His brother waved at him from across the room and he waved back, satisfied with his payback day.

Then, as if suddenly awakened from a dream, his brother's face dissolved into panic. He looked at his watch as he rushed over to the boy. It was easy to read the worry in the brother's eyes and the boy responded immediately to his brother's whispered instruction, to hurry home with him.

When they arrived at the house, their father was waiting by the window. His face, at first twisted in anger, slowly softened into relief. He wanted to know what they were thinking taking off like that. He wanted to know where they had been. Then the father sternly dismissed the boy, telling him to go to bed, and the serious discussion with his brother began.

The boy was in his bed listening but unable to really decipher the words. He glanced over at his brother's empty bed and felt a moment of pity. The day had been great. He had tasted beer, been to a party with girls, gone to the lake with older guys and ridden in a big black Mercury. Now, it was all going wrong. The boy had never seen his father so upset. He really wished he hadn't chosen the lake for his payback. He didn't think it would turn out to be such a big deal. If it hadn't been for those girls and that dumb party they would have made it home. He turned out his light but he couldn't sleep.

Get a Bigger Wagon

When the big brother came into their room and slipped into bed, the boy desperately wanted to talk to him and tell him he was sorry. He desperately wanted to know what had happened between his big brother and their father. Something, maybe respect, or maybe fear, kept him quiet.

No one in the family spoke about the incident the next day, or ever, for that matter. The boy noticed that it was several Saturdays before his brother went out with his friends again.

On this day I think my husband realized that payback can be a bittersweet thing. When I asked him what he learned from this experience he said, "Be careful what you wish for, because you just might get it." He added that those hasty "why not" decisions can lead you into a series of problems.

Big Business

The boy's mind was always active with plans to build something, make money or explore. Often he enjoyed the planning and anticipating, at least as much as he enjoyed reaching his goal. In small town Saskatchewan, in the late fifties, neighbors knew each other and the boy's neighbors knew he would respond with curiosity and enthusiasm, if they needed help with a task.

One hot July morning, a neighbor from a few doors down, asked the boy if he would be available to mow the grass and water the lawn for a couple of weeks. The neighbor would pay him when he returned. The weather would set his wage by determining the number of times the lawn would need to be cut and watered. After a few instructions, the boy and the neighbor shook hands and the agreement was in place.

The next day, the boy was busy pushing his own mower back and forth across the family lawn when another neighbor approached him with a lawn care request. This neighbor would be away for three weeks and he too, would pay the boy when he returned.

The message was as clear as the summer sky. The boy had a service to provide and people had a need for his service. He would start a lawn care business. He could handle several yards because he planned to be efficient. He could mow one yard and start watering it.

Get a Bigger Wagon

Then, he would mow another yard and run back every hour to move the sprinklers at the first house. By the time he was mowing the third yard, the first would be watered, and he would begin to water the second. The size of the yard would determine how many times the sprinklers would have to be moved and although no

plan could be perfect, he thought he had a pretty clear idea of how the business was going to run.

Each day he worked a while at the family store and he had some chores to do at home, but apart from that, he would concentrate fully on his lawn business. He estimated that he could take care of nine or ten lawns at one time. He was excited!

His parents were good friends with the neighbors who lived four doors north. The boy's mother often had coffee with the neighbor lady and the two couples enjoyed occasional meals and movies together. When the boy asked these neighbors about their lawn care needs, he was hired immediately! They were planning to leave for the lake the next morning. The boy could not believe how easy it was to grow a business.

Day after day, the boy's summer lawn care business operated just as he had planned. Most days he mowed and watered three yards. He enjoyed the work. As he pushed the mowers, he listened to the sound of the whirring blades and he enjoyed the pungent smell of the cut grass. Each customer's mower had its own sound. Each water sprinkler had its own mesmerizing swish.

One ordinary morning, during the summer of the lawn care business, he had completed the cutting of three yards and was almost finished watering the last. This lawn belonged to his parent's friends from four doors north. They were the only people he knew who had underground sprinklers. After cleaning the grass clippings out of the little cups that surrounded each sprinkler, he turned the taps on and watched the sprinkler heads jolt into action. The neighbor wasn't very happy with these sprinklers but the boy could only think about how easy it was to have no hoses to move. He was hot and thirsty and the rest of this watering would take care of itself, so he went home for a glass of water and some shade.

As he sat on the front step rubbing his tender upper arms and sipping water, he noticed two of his friends walking toward him. After the usual greetings and some discussion, they decided to go to the creek for the rest of the day. They would camp for the night and stay on if the weather was nice. The boy was glad he had his lawn care work caught up. His mother agreed to the outing and after a quick lunch he put a few items in a bag and headed out to meet his friends.

At the creek, the boys explored all of the usual places, prepared their campsite with careful precision and shared the food they had gathered from their homes. As they settled in for the evening, it began to rain. The soft mist soothed and revived the land. Raindrops tapped so gently on their roof that they were lulled into the deepest dreamiest sleep and just this once, while in a tent at the creek, the boys stayed asleep until morning.

When they wakened, they were surprised at how beautiful and new the creek appeared. The spider webs on the plants were wet and in the bright sunlight they looked like sculpted wire. The boys had never noticed this before and went closer to be sure that their eyes weren't deceiving them. They ate what was left of their food and they walked for miles.

While the boy enjoyed the creek, his mother was in the front yard, snipping beautiful fragrant roses for her kitchen table. She too, had enjoyed the gentle rain but she noticed that the dry prairie earth had already begun to greedily absorb the moisture. The sky today, was blue and cloud free.

Then she noticed water running down the street toward her house. She wondered where it could be coming from. She was annoyed that someone would waste so much water just to get a greener lawn. She would investigate.

After removing her apron and returning her shears to the kitchen, she began to follow the water's path. It led her toward her friend's house and the closer she got, the wider the stream became. When she reached their yard she was surprised to feel her feet sinking and sloshing through soggy lawn. She thought it rather odd that the sprinklers were active in spite of the steady rain they had enjoyed. Then, a sick feeling swept over her as she realized the boy must have forgotten to turn off the sprinklers before he left for the creek. As she turned the taps off, she became worried about the accumulation of water around the base of the house and in the hollows outside of the basement windows. She quickly went home for the key to her friend's house. She would check inside.

At the entrance to her neighbor's home, she took a deep breath, slowly turned the key and opened the door. Descending cautiously to the basement, she realized that a serious amount of water had seeped in. Walking through water a couple of inches deep, she opened the door to the linen closet and grabbed all of the dark towels. She began soaking up the water with them, carrying them, water laden, to the sink. It took all of her strength to wring them out. She gathered up newspapers and magazines that were too wet to save and placed them in an empty cardboard box. She took two damp mats to the sink, squeezed water out of them and took them outside to hang them on the clothesline. She was glad the couch and chairs were on six inch legs. The upholstery was still dry.

She took the towels home to wash and dry, and brought some of her own dark towels to continue mopping. The cleaning went on for several hours. In the end everything worked out fine but the boy would need to be made aware of his oversight. The consequences might have been much worse.

When the boy arrived home he was eagerly anticipating supper. He entered his home oblivious to the events he had triggered. His mother, as always, wanted to hear about his trip. As he headed to his room, he told her about the spider webs and the gentle rain and his wonderful sleep.

It was then that she asked him if he had forgotten to do anything before he left. An anxious sinking feeling came with the gradual realization that he maybe hadn't finished someone's yard. Then, as he thought, he remembered the yard with the underground sprinklers. Into his conscious mind, came an image of the sprinklers swirling from their metal cups. His eyes met his mother's and she knew by the anguished concern on his face that he understood. She didn't have to mention the responsibility that comes with running a business.

She told him that she was going to the neighbor's house to return the laundered towels. They would have supper as soon as she returned. He stood silent as she walked away. At least a week went by before he turned those sprinklers on again.

I have occasionally had to convince my husband that some business obligations will keep until after a vacation or an outing. I think experiences like this one, led him to believe that the old adage, business before pleasure, was in fact a truth. When I asked him what he learned from his lawn care business he said, "I learned that moms are great! Every businessman should be so lucky as to have one, to clean up his mistakes."

Bigger is Better

It was a summer afternoon in the late fifties and the
boy had just phoned a friend to come over to play. As
he waited in the backyard, he spread himself flat on the
damp grass, eyes toward the sky, and watched the clouds
moving, dividing and reforming. He thought about all
of the things that were changing. Everywhere in the
small Saskatchewan town, there was building going on.
He had often rafted on the slough and played Lone
Ranger in the trees, on the farm land that they were
now developing for houses. The boy decided he did not
mind change. In fact, change was exciting.

It was in this spirit of change that the boy turned
his head to one side and noticed the stash of lumber
beneath his patio. He guessed it must have been left
over from building the fence and trellis in the backyard. An idea began to develop immediately. The boy
and his friend could build a fort at the very back of
his yard where the trees would help conceal it. As the
friend approached, the boy jumped up to meet him and
explained his plan. The friend responded with enthusiasm and the two began hauling boards and tools to
their new job site.

They held boards for each other and hammered
and pieced small bits together to make walls. The scrap
pieces made for a weak structure and time and again it

collapsed under its own weight. After a frustrating afternoon, they could see that their fort lacked that certain professionalism. They agreed to meet after supper and do something about getting better materials.

That night they rode their bicycles through the new neighborhood and noticed there were no workmen in the area. There were, however, many pieces of wood flung haphazardly onto piles. They concluded that these pieces were likely too small for building homes. One project's waste could be another project's salvation. These pieces would do nicely for a fort. They rode their bikes back to the boy's yard, got the wagon and set out on foot to select appropriate building supplies for their project.

They chose pieces of plywood measuring about two feet by four feet. They even sourced useable two-by-fours. The fort would be strong and large with this new lumber. They stored their new supplies in the boy's yard and agreed to begin serious building in the coolness of the morning.

The morning was glorious and after big breakfasts the boys met and began their efforts. They wore gloves and stuck tools in their pockets and belts. The boy placed a pencil over his ear and held extra nails in his mouth. They knew they looked like every construction man in town. The fort was growing strong and straight by afternoon. They would soon need more materials. Although they were sure they were collecting scrap lumber, they decided to go in the evening to select more. For one thing, they wouldn't bother the workmen that way.

For several days they gathered supplies by night and did carpentry by day. They grew bolder about selecting the waste lumber and occasionally dragged home some larger pieces. The fort in the backyard grew bigger and bigger and seemed to be designing itself. Their friends came by often to admire their work. The boy's mother was completely unaware of the clandestine project taking place beyond the trees, right in her own backyard.

One night, as the boys made their materials selection, a truck came at them a little too fast, with its horn honking angrily. The boy, knowing deep down that his supply source was questionable, immediately dropped the lumber and did a complete one-eighty toward the trees, where they had played Lone Ranger just a summer ago. His friend, larger and slower than the boy, followed as swiftly as possible. The truck bounced violently over the ruts and ridges that once had been a ploughed field and an old slough. The boy glanced over his shoulder, feeling terror at being pursued by such an angry unrelenting adversary!

The whole evening had a nightmare quality, but in dreams the boy usually escaped by flying. This time he felt heavy and grounded. The man driving the old truck bounced around in the cab, banging his head repeatedly on the roof and looking angrier by the minute. The slower friend was all there was between the boy and the truck. As the truck gained on them, the boy got a glimpse of the driver and knew they were being chased by the foreman of the development.

The boy motioned to his friend to head toward the trees. They were planted tightly together to shelter the old farm, and the crazed builder would never be able to drive his truck through them. With every ounce of energy they had, the boy and his friend, ran through the trees and continued beyond them for some time. They hid in tall grass, panting for air, waiting until it seemed safe to head for home.

If the boy and his friend had thought for a moment, they would have known that the chase was merely the beginning of the end. After all, they had recognized the truck driver; it was likely that he had recognized them too.

In the morning, the man was at the boy's house before breakfast. He described the boy's method of selecting supplies as "theft" and he waved an angry finger at the boy's mother. He expected the lumber back, and he expected it nail free and soon! The boy's mother smiled calmly and assured him she would deal with the problem post haste! Then she wished him a good morning.

Having gone to the backyard to have a look at the fort, the mother asked the boy to sit with her for a moment. She mentioned that the boy and his friend had done a marvelous job of construction and that they definitely showed promise in the field. However, the lumber they had used, belonged to someone else, and he definitely wanted it back. She was very sorry, but the boy and his friend would have to un-build the fort immediately, and pay particular attention to removing all the nails.

So began one of the longest days the boy had ever experienced. The day was extremely hot and the work extremely physical. They drank buckets of water and even threw some on each other. It was much harder to remove a nail than to pound it in. Over and over again they hooked the pronged backs of their hammers under the nail heads, to pry the unwilling things from the wood. They wondered why they had built the fort so well.

After the evening meal, they began hauling the slabs of lumber back to the job site. They used the boy's wagon but still they made many trips. As they worked, they talked about how great their fort had been. To pass the time, they counted steps to and from the site. They made their last trip, as the stars began to shine. It was a beautiful night and the boy and his friend spread their weary bodies down on the damp cool grass and looked up at the clouds moving past the moon and the stars. They were still, for a while.

I knew my husband had built many businesses that had to, eventually, be abandoned or deconstructed. I thought he would tell me this experience might have taught him to rest-up and move on. When I asked him what he learned from his experience he said, "The price might seem right but always make sure your supplier is really on board."

Temptations

One Saskatchewan summer, in the late nineteen fifties, the boy met a band of adventurers living within one family. The four brothers, all a few years older or younger than the boy, lived several blocks from him. Each day, as he made the journey to their house, the boy anticipated the new and exciting adventure they would have. The boy became fast friends with the two brothers closest to his own age. The summer was filled with climbing forbidden piles of lumber, biking miles through and around the entire town, building and floating rafts and raiding gardens. It was a time of exciting close calls. The boy came to understand feelings of camaraderie and loyalty. He would have stood by the brothers no matter what the challenge.

These warm golden summer days ran together in the boy's mind like scenes from a good movie. Before long, fall arrived. It was time to buy school supplies and rake leaves.

On the first day of school, the bell rang to call the children into class and everyone knew summer was officially over. The boy knew from experience that there would still be time to have adventures after school and on Saturdays. What he didn't know was that summer relationships can be forgotten as quickly as the leaves turn from green to burnt orange.

Get a Bigger Wagon

It all began when the after-school bell rang announcing the end of the first day. There was a new guy in class who was a good talker and he quickly found the brothers on the playground both at noon and at recess. He captivated them with stories of his adventures in his previous town.

After school, as the boy approached the group to confirm the usual meeting place over at the fields, he heard the new guy inviting the brothers to the Texaco, promising to buy them each a hamburger. The boy wanted to get started on a new project. He assumed the invitation to go for a hamburger included him so it was with great confidence that he suggested they all go to the fields instead. There was really only an hour until everyone's mom would have a warm supper ready. Sidetracked for a moment, he let his mind imagine the taste of his mother's homemade spaghetti and crusty rolls. He loved the feeling of being ravenous followed by the incredible joy of the first bite of one of his mom's delicious meals.

As the boy had this private thought, the brothers started walking with the new guy towards the Texaco. As they departed, they indicated to the boy that they would see him later. It slowly and painfully occurred to him that he wasn't invited to go for hamburgers. A feeling of tightness began to grip his chest and he became aware of his heart throbbing in his ears. He stood silent, arms hanging limply by his sides, trying to grasp what had just happened.

After a few minutes, he turned and walked slowly toward his dad's store. The cool breeze was welcome on his hot cheeks. At the store he quietly swept the sidewalk and polished the windows. As he worked, he felt his sadness fade. After closing the store, he and his father rode home to the warm inviting smells of their family kitchen.

As they ate supper together, he learned that his dad had met the new guy's father. Apparently, the new guy's mother had moved somewhere without them. His father made good money, but the job required travel. The boy would be staying with neighbors much of the time.

The brothers and the new guy seemed inseparable for a few weeks. Then, one day when the snow was falling into heavy wet piles, the brothers suggested to the boy that they meet at the fields after school. The boy agreed to the plan. No one mentioned the new guy, or where he was on that day. The brothers and the boy built snow forts and threw snowballs. After an hour of rigorous snow play, they ran home for warm suppers feeling delightfully ravenous. Things felt sort of familiar.

The brothers and the boy laughed together that day and occasionally over the months that followed. However, for the boy, the magic of the summer of the brothers was only a memory. The boy was less innocent. He knew that something as small as a free hamburger could change important plans.

My husband values loyalty above most other traits in a human being. When he makes a decision in business, loyalty is given more weight than financial savings. When I asked him what he learned from this experience, he said, "I learned that few friendships are able to withstand life's challenges long enough to mature into forever friendships." Then he added, "I also came to realize how expensive free hamburgers can be."

You First

A few miles away from the small prairie town, a thin creek ran through a wide valley. Small boys made journeys to this valley to explore, have adventures and challenge each other, in order to practice being the men they would one day become.

One day, in late spring, the sun warmed the pavement of the highway out of town and the boy and two of his more occasional friends set out to the creek. They rode their bicycles and had one canvas bag in tow. In the bag was a canteen of water, a couple tins of brown beans, a dull can opener and three old spoons. The boy had a small box of matches in his pocket that he had scooped from his father's ashtray, on the way out the door. He kept these matches hidden knowing the other boys likely had some useful supplies as well. There was prestige in being casually prepared.

They searched for arrow heads and old bones and made up stories about people who had lived and died near the creek. They found an old bottle, a rubber boot and a stone that might have been a tool long ago. They opened the beans when they were hungry and took turns scooping mounds into their mouths with their spoons.

There was a bridge over the creek and sometimes the spring run-off swelled the little creek right up to the crossing. One year, water actually flooded over the bridge. On this day, the boys were able to sit under the bridge to get cool when the sun got high and hot. The air under the bridge was damp and their faces felt refreshed. The smell was bitter and wet like used tea leaves. The boy liked the smell. He inhaled deeply and felt peaceful.

Then the afternoon took an unforgettable turn. One of the boy's friends noticed an abundance of frogs lazing in the same cool area. With one inexplicable thought wave, the friend pulled a knife from his pocket and announced that he would catch and kill some frogs. The boy never even got a chance to ask why. The friend quickly went on to explain that in some parts of the world eating frogs' legs was popular. Some primitive hunter instinct had clearly overtaken this friend.

The boy felt immediately queasy but there was little time to dwell on this feeling because it took his friend only moments to kill and ready two rather large frogs with the knife. The three boys looked down at the four repulsive legs, severed from their frog bodies. If they thought about how fragile life was, no one mentioned it. If they were nauseous, no one admitted it. There was a moment of quiet, not out of respect, but out of confusion. Each boy waited for someone to suggest how the feast should be prepared.

Finally, the hunter-friend outlined a plan. An empty bean tin would hold water that they could boil over a fire. They would toss the legs into this boiling water to cook them until they were tender. The boy had matches and wondered if either of his friends did. He contemplated keeping them to himself. However, when the question was asked, each boy searched his pockets and at last the boy produced his box of wooden matches. This at least made him look like an enthusiastic participant.

So the fire was lit, the tin was filled with canteen water and placed in the flames and when the water began to boil the wretched legs were assembled near the pot. It had to be decided who should go first. There were no volunteers. The hunter-friend decided that they would need to draw straws. There was a great deal of discussion while three straws of varying lengths were selected. Then, three better straws were selected. There was discussion about how one boy would hold the straws and he would take whatever straw was left after the other two had drawn. The short straw would eat first. By now, it was clear that even the hunter didn't really want to eat the loathsome delicacy. However, once a plan takes form, it has a life of its own. The friends had become trapped in their own adventure. The legs were dropped into the boiling water.

Now, the boy and the hunter painstakingly selected a straw from the hand of the third friend. No one looked until the drawing was finished. The decision was clear and the hunter uttered a prolonged groan, pulled his knife from his pants and fished a droopy leg from the pot. He swiftly lifted the flimsy flesh, overcooked and offensive, toward his mouth and made short work of his short straw selection.

When it was the boy's turn he knew that it was best to swallow it quickly. Still, part of him wanted to keep it in his mouth long enough to discover how it would taste. As he lifted the tiny morsel to his mouth he noticed the skin had peeled away and the flesh did look cooked. It appeared sticky and as he put it in his mouth he felt his stomach lurch and it was clear that he should swallow it immediately.

Their task complete, the friends put the fire out with creek water and felt the surge of adrenaline that always follows accomplishment. There would be plenty of time to think about what they had done. For now, they would pedal energetically from the joy of relief. It was the longest meal any of them had ever experienced. The actual eating took sixty seconds, but the deciding who would go first, took almost an hour.

I know that on these outings, my husband learned to keep his fears and insecurities to himself, while testing his capacity to handle unpalatable situations. When I asked him what he thought he learned on this day, he said, "I learned that if you are going to follow someone, you should make sure he isn't an idiot and most importantly, that he's willing to go first."

The Hillman

On the outskirts of the small Saskatchewan town, there was an acreage with many buildings and interesting animals. Parked in the grassy yard, as if it still intended to arrive somewhere, was an old Hillman with red leather seats. The boy knew every abandoned vehicle for miles around the town because as much as he enjoyed riding his bike, he enjoyed stopping to explore. This car demanded more of his time each visit. One day, he asked the owner if he could sit in the car and permission was cheerfully given.

The boy opened the door and slid into the well worn driver's seat. He adjusted the rear view mirror and he glanced casually over his shoulder. He knew he looked good in the car. He pulled his sunglasses from his jacket pocket and put them on with one hand as he steadied the steering wheel with the other. He rolled down the window and placed his elbow casually on the lip of the door, allowing his arm to drape through the open window. He gave a little wave to the tree as though it was a friend crossing the street. The steering wheel was bound in leather and almost overfilled his grip. As he reluctantly got out of the car, the owner waved at him and told him to come back anytime.

The smell of the car varied with the weather. Warm sun made it smell new and leathery. Cold winds made it smell more like the thickening oil in its engine. That summer the boy had many adventures while sitting inside the abandoned car. One day, as he waved to the owner from the car window, he thought he heard the man tell him he could have the car if he could get it started. The boy's green eyes were open as wide as his mouth when the man confirmed the offer by handing him the keys. After a few seconds, he stammered a breathless thank you and sat quietly wondering what to do next. The boy decided that just in case the owner was wrong about the car being out of commission, he should try the keys in the ignition. Twice he turned the

key and gave it a little gas. Nothing happened. In his single decade on earth, the boy learned that, more often than not, a car that wouldn't start simply needed a new battery. He pedaled home energetically. He would own the car!

First, he counted the money in his piggy bank. He did this almost every Sunday. The bank didn't have a removable bottom so he had learned to pump a kitchen knife in and out of the slot, while holding the ceramic pig upside down and slightly tilted. This brought a parade of coins to their edges as they streamed right past the knife and out of the bank. He had plenty of cash. The next day he would discuss his battery needs with the automotive manager at the hardware store.

In the morning, the boy bought the battery and, as the clerk handed it to him, he felt the dense weight of the thing. He knew then, that he should have brought his wagon. He considered going home for it but the anticipation of owning a car was too strong to ignore. He began the long walk to the acreage on the outskirts of town. He chose to take a shortcut down a back street across the schoolyard and over the highway. The crescent wrench he carried in his belt bounced annoyingly against the back of his leg and the bottom edge of the battery cut cruelly into his fingers. Sweat began to run into his eyes. His shoulders felt like they were separating from his back. Queasiness was growing in his stomach and he found himself falling forward into each step rather than having control over his progress. Just as he was about to drop the battery, he managed to set it down on the grass at the edge of the schoolyard. He wiped his eyes with his sleeve and thought for a minute about how he could get this job done.

He decided he would have to put the battery down every fifty steps. The plan worked because the counting took his mind off the pain which now enveloped his small frame. Fifty steps and a rest, fifty steps and a rest, on and on for thousands of steps and then forty-eight, forty-nine, fifty and he saw the Hillman. He stumbled faster into a clumsy run and laboriously covered the last few yards. He put the battery down, wiped his face on his sleeve and focused on the task at hand.

Alone, he lifted the hood, wrenched the bolts loose, replaced the battery and closed the hood. With a smile of satisfaction, he slid into his car and confidently put the key in the ignition. The motor complained twice and then jolted into action. He put the car in gear, as his father had shown him, and slowly gave it some gas. With the sheer joy of accomplishment he drove his own car across the large yard. It occurred to him that he should inform the owner that he was taking the car as per their agreement. He made a wide turn and headed back toward the buildings. Then, like it was tired, the Hillman ground to a slow and gentle stop in almost exactly the same spot it had occupied for several years. It would take a discerning individual to notice that the car had been driven because the only change in the scene was that it now faced the opposite direction.

The boy knew he owned the car because he had started it. He wasn't sure why it had stopped. As he raised his eyes, he saw the nearby auto body shop and decided he would ask them to take a look at his car.

If the workers at the shop found him amusing as he asked them to come and take a look at his car, they never showed it on their faces. They took the boy with them as they went with a tow truck to collect the Hillman. Back at the shop they gave the car a thorough investigation and then informed the boy that his car had a crack in the block. It really was basically useless.

After a moment of silence, the boy asked what they would give him for it. The men did some serious calculating and came up with twenty dollars as a firm offer. The boy looked up at the men, carefully disguised his excitement and seriously counter-offered, telling them that it was a deal as long as he got his battery back. The agreement was made.

After the battery was removed from the Hillman and the twenty dollars was paid to the boy, everyone shook hands. The boy picked up the battery and began the strenuous journey back to the hardware store. Once again, he broke the trip into pain-filled intervals of fifty steps each, counting to distract himself. Again, he was plagued by the crescent wrench banging against his leg, the searing pain in his arms and now the gnawing need for food and water.

The clerk at the hardware store knew the boy well and he could see the exhaustion in his stance. Man to man, and likely against company policy, the battery with the receipt was exchanged for cash. The walk home was about a mile but without the battery in his hands it seemed insignificant. The boy used the time to savor the details of his full and profitable day.

Get a Bigger Wagon

I know the owner was glad to get the car removed at no cost to him. The auto body shop might have made a little on parts and scrap metal. The boy had extra cash in his pocket. In the end, everyone involved got something. I saw this story as an illustration of the win-win theory.

When I asked my husband what he learned that day, he said, "I learned to always make the best of a disappointing situation. Things rarely turn out exactly as we plan them." After a few minutes of introspection he told me once more how much he had loved sitting in that car and how it taught him that great pleasure can be found in not even moving.

If we need a bigger wagon, it's because ours is full of gratitude to everyone who helped with this project.

The boy grew up and became an entrepreneur, partly because his parents didn't over-parent him. When he became a man, he married a woman, who had developed a love of paper, ink, words and printing presses when she was a little girl, living with her entrepreneurial parents. The man told his wife many stories from his childhood and she began to write them down and put them in a book. They knew an artist named Denyse Klette who agreed, in spite of having the busiest year of her artistic life, to paint pictures to go with the stories and to oversee the processes to make them print-ready. The artist knew a boy named Aidan Stubbs who looked a bit like the man did, when he was a boy. Aidan posed tirelessly, replicating the boy's actions in the stories and Shannon Brunner, of n.y.snaps, took pictures of him so that Denyse could get the paintings just right. Les Weinrichson digitally photographed most of the finished paintings, with Shannon capturing some. Chelsea Klette and Curtis Rostad did digital clean-up readying the illustrations for printing. During this time, Mr. Geoff Bjorgan, of the Book and Brier Patch, frequently gave the man and the woman encouragement and wise advice and agreed to help them promote and launch the book in Regina. Tammy McCumber and Paula Woodhouse of The Giggle Factory supplied encouragement and introduced the woman to Christine Lyon, editor of Saskatoon Lifestyle Magazine, and she published some of the *Get a Bigger Wagon* stories. She needed a picture of the man and the woman so Dennis and Sheila Evans of Picture Perfect Portraits arranged for Rachel Duquette to do an emergency shoot early one morning. Whenever the man or the woman felt discouraged, Denyse would ask Dinah Raine to read a story and, if she laughed or cried or asked for more, they felt encouraged. Nicole Kozar spent hours editing and she was named editor-in-chief because, although many other people contributed in this area, it was Nicole who cheerfully went over every word several times. Chad Kozar listened patiently as his wife read the stories aloud and talked on the phone endlessly during the editing process. Michelle and Brett Pawson handled the woman's every computer crisis and listened enthusiastically when she read her stories. Deneen Gudjonson, of McNally Robinson Booksellers in Saskatoon, agreed to have an event to promote the book in Saskatoon. When Geoff Bjorgan invited the man and the woman to quickly get their book cover to a magic billboard creator, they were very glad that Curtis Rostad of Trafick IMS was quick to respond, as he has been with other support materials. He worked closely with Denyse to get the cover art ready. Michelle Boulton of Michelle Communications prepared the layout of stories and paintings for the book and helped the man and the woman smoothly work out several other details. Lyle Boulton of PrintWest Communications coordinated the printing process and many talented hands worked on printing the book once it was inside the big double doors on Miller Avenue. When three and a half year old Jarrett Pawson, grandson of the man and the woman, learned that the book was dedicated to him, he asked if they could fax him that information so he could have it in writing. Everyone is still smiling.

About the Author

M aureen Haddock was born into a printing family
and spent much of her early childhood with her
parents in their Manitoba weekly newspaper office. At
the time, her parents were the youngest publishers in
Manitoba. Her love of the printed word grew from these
stimulating surroundings.

Maureen received her Bachelor of Education from
the University of Saskatchewan in 1970 and, later the
same year, married her entrepreneurial childhood sweet-
heart. A talented writer and educator, Maureen has
distinguished herself in the fields of communications,
training, creative services and writing. She has used all
of these skills in the many businesses she and her husband have shared.

Her previously published or recorded writings
include: short stories, poetry, song lyrics, newspaper
columns, publicity material, scripts for DVD and CD, as
well as educational materials for The
Body Shop Saskatchewan and The
Belly Button Buddies. At
present, she is co-writing
scripts for Shangers Ltd.
(a British entertainment
company) and writing
another book.

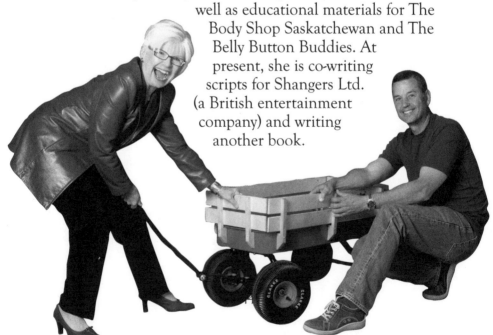

About The Artist

Denyse Klette was the perfect choice when it came to selecting an artist to portray the boy in this book. Denyse, like the boy, has a fiercely entre-preneurial streak that has remained intact since childhood. She loved the stories and had an immediate understanding of the boy's nature.

Although she has worked in many art mediums and can paint in many styles, she chose to capture the era for this book by using a soft monochromatic presentation, remi-niscent of daydreams, memories and the early days of television. Then, she called upon her experi-ence as a portrait artist to depict the detailed emotion in the boy's face. The resulting paintings make viewers feel like they have just stepped into someone's memory.

For information about Denyse Klette and the many projects she is involved with, please visit www.dklette.com.